GROW UP
ALREADY!

GROW UP ALREADY!

PRACTICAL WAYS TO BECOME MATURE IN CHRIST THROUGH THE POWER OF THE HOLY SPIRIT

DR. MARITZA RIVERA

TABLE OF CONTENTS

ACKNOWLEDGMENTS

ХХ

To Dad – You are the person who taught me what it meant to live a Holy Spirit guided life. You exemplified a Christ-like maturity. I miss you every day. See you in heaven.

Mom – Thank you. You have influenced my walk in Christ to such an extent that I am who I am today because you and Dad chose to follow Jesus. I'm thankful for your love, prayers, care, and sacrifices.

Omar and my beautiful children, Caleb and Keila – You all remind me daily of the blessings of God in my life. I'm grateful for your love, understanding, prayers, and continued support.

PROLOGUE

✕

As a schoolteacher, Friday, March 13, 2020, is a day that I remember vividly. There was a buzz in the air about a thing called COVID-19 as the school day began. I had heard about it in the news in previous days, but in all honesty, I never considered it would make it out to where I am from in Chicago, Illinois. As the day progressed, the concept of imminent shutdown became a likely reality as emails and chatter filled the atmosphere. "Please prepare some E-learning plans." "Please send electronic devices home with students." Eventually, I received the formal email from the district superintendent titled, "District Closed Next Week." In ignorance I thought that we would be back at work in a week or so. Unbeknown to many of us, it would become a very overwhelming period in history.

Alongside being an educator, I am also a pastor. I have been leading worship and teaching the word for a long time. Everyone was navigating new ground during the pandemic, trying to figure out what to do next; the church was no exception. We were making day-to-day decisions and were constantly re-evaluating them. There was so much uncertainty. I kept asking myself, Are we doing the right thing? What should we do now? All the questions that could come to mind did come to my mind.

We worked on a plan and soon enough we began to live stream a church service with worship and word three days a week. We live streamed prayer services on social media to pray for one another. We had Bible studies on Zoom. We even did outdoor services. The crew would arrive early in the morning and set everything up outside on our newly constructed, outdoor stage. We did everything we could to keep our church engaged and growing in the Lord. Eventually – and thank God – we were able to reopen completely.

COVID-19 affected everyone physically, emotionally, and spiritually. The time of quarantine changed everything. But there was something else that this quarantine offered to us – the opportunity for self-reflection. As I self-reflected, I realized there was a struggle for my faith during the pandemic. I faced trials and tribulations. I faced some of the most difficult moments of my life. But I had a decision to make. I could come out of this quarantine one of three ways – I could get stagnant, I could shrink back, or I could mature. I chose the latter. I wanted to be a grown up.

The truth is we all are affected by life circumstances. It is not just about the Pandemic of 2020. It is about all the things that hit us in life – our broken marriages, struggles with our children, the loss of a loved one, the overwhelming sense of loneliness, or even the loss of hope. We are all confronted with trials and tribulations because we live in a broken world.

So, then what makes any difference if we are all to be affected by life? To me, the difference is clear: the most contributing factor that produced maturity in the midst of adversity was a relationship with the Holy Spirit.

I'll give you a warning now, this book will push you, challenge you, and stretch you. It is going to compel you to walk deeper in the Lord, to give up the things that weigh you down, and to make some challenging life changes, but it will all be better for you. You can begin to walk in the freedom that comes from maturity in the Spirit.

CHAPTER ONE

GROWING OUT OF INFANCY

ХХ

When I was a child, I spoke and thought and
reasoned as a child. But when I grew up,
I put away childish things.

1 Corinthians 13:11 NLT

It is as if, in this verse, Paul, the author of the book of 1 Corinthians, is speaking to the church of the twenty-first cen-
tury. He is addressing the constant goal of the local and global
church—to grow out of childish behaviors and into spiritual
maturity. To preach with the power and authority of the Holy
Spirit so that the hearers of the word would be transformed
into mature Christians has been the major focus of the local
pastor for centuries.

According to Strong's Exhaustive Concordance of the Bible, the word child in the preceding verse, 1 Corinthians 13:11, is defined as "a simple-minded person; an immature Christian." In other words, immaturity is the state of not being fully grown. Immaturity is a stage of infancy.

In 1 Corinthians 3:1-3, Paul makes a clear distinction between a childish, immature Christian and a spiritually mature Christian. A few years prior to writing these verses, Paul had spent eighteen months with the church of Corinth, and just a few years later, he was admonishing them for their lack of spiritual growth. Paul had a clear expectation of what the growth of the "brethren" or Christians in the church of Corinth should have looked like, and he clearly spells it out.

> *And I, brethren, could not speak to you as to spiritual people but as to carnal, as to babes in Christ. I fed you with milk and not with solid food; for until now you were not able to receive it, and even now you are still not able; for you are still carnal. For where there are envy, strife, and divisions among you, are you not carnal and behaving like mere men? (1 Corinthians 3:1-3 NKJV)*

These attributes can be applied to our own lives.

Spiritual

Mature brethren in the faith are referred to as "spiritual". According to Vine's Expository Dictionary, the word "spiritual" here is a word that is an "after-Pentecost word". This word is not found in the Gospels. However, we do continue to find this word throughout some of the remaining books of the New Testament, particularly in connection with the Holy Spirit. In

Galatians 5:25, Paul describes those who are spiritual as those who "walk in the spirit". From this, we can conclude that this word "spiritual" is meant to be a descriptive word that represents the power of the Holy Spirit working in our lives to bring us to a level of being spiritual. So to be considered mature, we must also be walking in the Spirit.

Immature believers are the exact opposite. Paul refers to them as "carnal,"[1] referring to the flesh. The New Living Translation (NLT) refers to carnal as being "controlled by the flesh". The New International Version (NIV) equates it to being "worldly". These are all strong descriptions for someone who Paul begins addressing as "brethren,"[2] but the reality is that we are warned over and over again throughout scripture how the flesh interferes with our spiritual growth.

Can you just imagine if a pastor today called some of his congregants babies or carnal? I'm sure some of the church folk would walk out never to return.

I grew up in a strong, Bible-based church where my father was the pastor. His teachings remind me of Paul. My father had an encounter much like Paul, one that turned him completely around. When my father gave his life to Jesus, he gave his whole life to Jesus. He stopped drinking, and he stopped smoking. He walked, talked, and exemplified Christ. He was a straightforward, no-nonsense guy. He taught with love and authority. I am grateful for the strong words preached that compelled me to live for Jesus, for it produced in me a maturity. I learned that, if you want to grow out of that infancy, you can't get offended when a preacher preaches a strong word that convicts you.

---

1   1 Corinthians 3:3 New King James Version.
2   1 Corinthians 3:1 New King James Version.

Solid Food

Mature brethren in the faith are referred to as those who can receive "solid food". Solid food can only be digested by a mature individual. One of the most compelling passages of the Bible that explains this concept can be found in Hebrews 5:12-14.

> *For though by this time you ought to be teachers, you need someone to teach you again the first principles of the oracles of God; and you have come to need milk and not solid food. For everyone who partakes only of milk is unskilled in the word of righteousness, for he is a babe. But solid food belongs to those who are of full age, that is, those who by reason of use have their senses exercised to discern both good and evil (Hebrews 5:12-14 NKJV).*

Paul goes on to refer to the immature as those who continue to drink milk when they should be eating solid foods. It is not just that they are incapable of digesting solid food; it is that there were things that prevented them from receiving the Word of God, digesting it, and applying it to their lives. Those that drink milk are spiritual infants, immature in many ways. Infants lack many of the basic abilities needed to eat a solid meal. A striking phrase in 1 Corinthians 3:2 is the description of the immature as "not being able to receive it." To say someone can receive solid food is to say they are at a level where they can take in what is being preached, taught, or revealed from the Word of God that then impacts how they think, behave, react, walk, talk, worship, and more. There is evidence of transformation.

Behavior

Mature brethren in the faith are controlled by the Holy Spirit. Their behavior is reflective of the Spirit's transformation in their life. A mature Christian allows the Holy Spirit to change their sinful nature.

> The Spirit begins this transformation in our lives the moment we come to know Jesus, and that transformation continues throughout our lives.

In their book *The New Christian Counselor*, Hawkins and Clinton state:

> The Holy Spirit enters the core self to regenerate and to animate the life of the human spirit. In his coming there is the power to overcome sin, to bring light where darkness has dominated, to commence the process of the restoration of the image of God in the core self, and to provide the energy and empowerment to obey the Word of God and reshape self in all its relationships from the inside out. The Holy Spirit is received through the gospel message by humans in need of redemption. This redemption has the power to set free those who are captive to sin and to the self. It frees humanity to make choices that lead to restoration of the image of God in the core self and weaken the power of sin in its desire to dominate the human will.

Immature Christians continue to struggle with childish behaviors and become stuck. We can see that the church of Corinth was stuck at the same level. In the book, *The Complete Guide to the Bible,* author Stephen M. Miller explains that Paul had spent over a year and a half building up the church of Corinth, which was far more than the time he had spent in other towns. Yet, there was no growth. Paul calls them "mere men," indistinguishable from the world. Their flesh is constantly in control, thus denying the Holy Spirit control over their life, and in turn creating a cycle of behaviors that stew on deep-seated issues, resulting in immaturity. The very thing that causes them to remain stagnant in a state of immaturity is the very thing they continue to feed on.

I remember a skit that a sister in church acted out for one of our church services. I must have been in my teen years—a long, long time ago. She came out dressed and acting like a baby with a bottle in her hand. I don't remember much after that, but I do know that the object of the skit was to make us see how silly it was for a full-grown adult to be acting like an infant.

As a teacher, I am very familiar with the stages of development for each grade level. There is a natural growth cycle. An infant becomes a child who becomes an adolescent who becomes an adult. Bear with me as I break it down academically and spiritually.

As a young teacher still learning about children and their stages of learning and development, I was encouraged by my professors to read up on psychologist Jean Piaget who was at the forefront of how children develop. Developing is part of the growth process and Piaget breaks things down into four stages. Each stage transitions into the next. These four stages are Sensorimotor from birth to 2, the Preoperational from age 2 to 7, the Concrete Operational from 7 to 11, and Formal Operational from age 11 and on.

The main idea was that children learn and develop in stages and that for them to move to the next stage they have to first reach maturity in their current stage (Lerner and Johns). This idea of stages in our development is a concept that has been introduced previously. The Scripture speaks of a spiritual development that is similar to the stages above. But instead of those hard educational terms above, Paul breaks them down into very simple terms.

The stages Paul uses in the Bible also follow a development that moves us from infancy to maturity—the new birth or born again stage (1 Peter 1:23), infancy and child stage (1 Corinthians 3:1; Ephesians 4:14; Hebrews 5:13), and ultimately, a maturing stage (Ephesians 4:13). This spiritual development is necessary for the Christian to develop out of infancy and into maturity.

New Birth

According to scripture, our spiritual development starts with a "new birth" or being "reborn".[3] John 1:12-13 NLT explains, *"But to all who believed him and accepted him, he gave the right to become children of God. They are reborn—not with a physical birth resulting from human passion or plan, but a birth that comes from God."* We also see the notion of a new birth in Titus 3:5 NLT: *"He washed away our sins, giving us a new birth and new life through the Holy Spirit."*

Unlike the actual day you were physically born, you probably remember the day you gave your life to Jesus. I imagine it was a wonderful experience for you. The freedom you felt by surrendering to God—that was your new birth. It wasn't physical;

---

3   John 1:12-13 New Living Translation.

it was a spiritual birth. That day, you finally felt the hope that Jesus offers. That was the start of your spiritual journey, the start of your life as a Christian.

Infancy

After a new birth, the initial stage of Christianity is referred to as infancy. The spiritual stage of infancy begins with a "new birth" and "new life". The old is gone; the new begins. We do not walk as before, but it is more than that. We are also experiencing a new life through the Holy Spirit. When a child is born, the parents are gentle and careful, yet fully expecting for the child to show signs of growth appropriate to the child's development. A parent expects that their child will reach developmental milestones like all other infants. Similarly, the Father is also expecting signs of growth as we begin to know Him. We grow in faith. We grow in love. We grow in the knowledge of the Word. WE GROW.

Maturity

The final stage is referred to as mature. A child is born. A child grows. A child becomes an adult. In their adulthood, an individual shows an ability to behave in a way that is appropriate to the scriptures. We will explore this topic more in the next chapter.

Many immature believers are stuck in the never-ending cycle of infancy. This is what Paul is talking about when he says to leave the childish things behind. "*When I was a child, I talked like a child, I thought like a child, I reasoned like a child. When I became a man, I put the ways of childhood behind me*" (1 Cor. 13:11 NIV). There is a clear contrast between a child and an adult, both physically and spiritually. There comes a time in our spiritual walk where we must decide to leave our infantile behaviors and GROW UP. In the next section, we will explore what we need to do to reach a greater level of spiritual maturity.

CHAPTER TWO

GROWING INTO MATURITY

)|(

"Solid food is for those who are mature,
who through training have the skill to recognize
the difference between right and wrong."

Hebrews 5:14 NLT

Have you ever found yourself spiritually stuck and unable to move forward? A lot of Christians get stuck in the monotony of life and have no idea what to do to get out of the never-ending cycle. As a pastor, teacher, and counselor, I have seen countless individuals make awful decisions out of the frustration of feeling stuck. They feel stuck, so they make changes that they think will 'unstuck' them. But often, these changes had impending consequences that brought on a whole new set of struggles.

What was the difference between those Christians who became stronger through adversity versus those that became weaker when faced with trials? What are the practices of certain Christians that afforded them a stronger, deeper spiritual life in Christ? As we discussed earlier, those that could stand strong in their faith demonstrated maturity, and those that could not demonstrated immaturity, as Paul mentioned in 1 Corinthians 3.

A 2018 study by Lifeway Research titled "How to Raise Spiritually Mature and Mentally Healthy Kids" explores five practices that were more likely to develop spiritual maturity. The study found that, "In addition to regularly reading the Bible, children who regularly prayed growing up, served in the church, listened primarily to Christian music, and participated in mission trips were more likely to still be spiritually healthy and active as an adult." The key takeaway from this study is that those that do all five of the above actions have a greater chance of stability and maturity in the Lord. These five practices can be adapted to Christians of all age groups, leading to growth and maturity[4].

Regularly reading the Bible.
Regularly praying.
Serving in the church.
Listening to Christian music.
Participating in missions.

In a small, anonymous 2022 study, I asked men and women questions about their faith to see how it lined up with the above study. Most (53%) of those who took the survey became Christians in their adolescent years between the ages of 5 to 12. Still others (23%) became Christians in their young adult

4   Earls, Aaron. 2019. "How to Raise Spiritually Mature And Mentally Healthy Kids – Lifeway Research". Lifeway Research. https://lifewayresearch. com/2018/09/24/how-to-raise-spiritually-mature-and-mentally-healthy-kids/

years between the ages of twenties or thirties. Surprisingly, only between 3% and 4% of those who had taken the survey became Christian in their adult years of fourties or older. (For more info on the study see appendix A.)

This anonymous study looked at five areas of maturity labeled by the Lifeway study mentioned earlier, and below is a summary of the results.

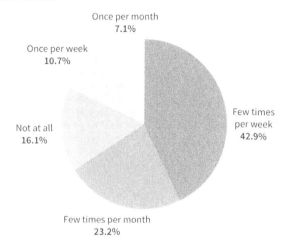

The statistics above are the answers given in general by all participants who labeled themselves as either 'baby Christians', 'struggling Christians', 'Christians', or 'mature Christians' (Appendix A for more details). When we solely looked at those in the study that labeled themselves as 'mature Christians' and their Bible reading habits, here's what was discovered:

Regularly Reading the Bible

When it came to regularly reading the Bible, overall, the study showed that in fact, 70% of mature Christians read their Bible a few times per week, proving that consistent Bible reading and maturity, have a mutual relationship. Some might even say that the cause of their maturity can be directly attributed to reading their Bible consistently. Of course, as Christians, we can understand the power of the Word of God to change our behaviors, transform our minds, and speak to our spirit. Every day we read the Word, we are filling ourselves with truth and erasing the devil's lies. Every day we read the Word, we are solidifying our identity in Christ. The Word is like water to a dry plant.... Without water, the plant dies. With water – the Word of God – our soul is nourished and lives.

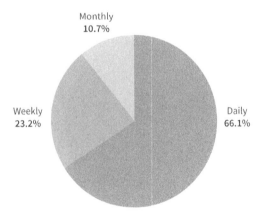

The statistics above are the answers given in general by all participants who labeled themselves as either 'baby Christians', 'struggling Christians', 'Christians', or 'mature Christians' (Appendix A for more details). When we solely looked at those in the study that labeled themselves as 'mature Christians' and their prayer habits, here's what was discovered:

Regularly Praying

When it came to regularly praying, overall, the study showed that in fact, 83% of those who consider themselves mature Christians, prayed daily. That means every day! This shows, once again, that there's a direct connection between daily prayer and spiritual maturity. As stated earlier, perhaps spiritual maturity can be directly attributed to praying consistently. Prayer is having conversations with God. It is deliberately making time to communicate with our Creator. As we communicate we learn who He is. A stronger bond is formed with Him. Our relationship is forged in our prayer time. It is no wonder that maturity comes out of the time we spend with Him for we become like Him as we spend time with Him. No, we don't become God, but His glory will rub off on us, much like how Moses' face was radiant after spending time with God.

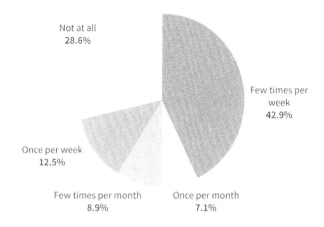

The statistics above are the answers given in general by all participants who labeled themselves as either 'baby Christians', 'struggling Christians', 'Christians', or 'mature Christians' (Appendix A for more details). When we solely looked at those in the study that labeled themselves as 'mature Christians' and their volunteer habits at their home church, here's what was discovered:

Serving in the Church

When it comes to serving in the church, I asked a question of participants who considered themselves mature Christians. The question was how often they served in the church. Not surprisingly, the data shows that there is a connection between being a mature believer and consistently serving in the church. We see that 66% of mature believers served in the church not just occasionally, but rather a few times per week. This has great implications for Christians everywhere. We can't say that everyone serving the church is a mature believer, but we can definitely see that with maturity comes a sense of responsibility in the kingdom of God, serving others, and serving in the church.

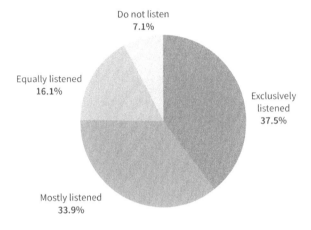

The statistics above are the answers given in general by all participants who labeled themselves as either 'baby Christians', 'struggling Christians', 'Christians', or 'mature Christians' (Appendix A for more details). When we solely looked at those in the study that labeled themselves as 'mature Christians' and their music listening habits, here's what was discovered:

Listening to Christian Music

In the next category, we asked about Christian music. And once again, breaking down the statistics, we take a closer look at those who only labeled themselves as mature Christians. The statistics showed that both these groups listen to Christian music almost exclusively or exclusively at an extraordinary 87.5%. As we look at all of the questions asked, we see a pattern in how mature believers walk in their faith. As we look at this particular area, we can see that as believers mature they choose to surround themselves with things that glorify God. But I also think that this particular point goes deeper into the concept of worship.

Mature believers are hungry for all things God and so they choose to listen to lyrics and music that places God at the center, reminds them of His goodness, and breathes life into their spirit.

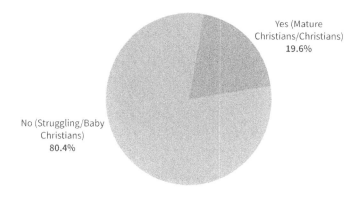

Yes (Mature Christians/Christians)
19.6%

No (Struggling/Baby Christians)
80.4%

The statistics above are the answers given in general by all participants who labeled themselves as either 'baby Christians', 'struggling Christians', 'Christians', or 'mature Christians' (Appendix A for more details). When we solely looked at those in the study that labeled themselves as 'mature Christians' and missions, here's what was discovered:

Participating in Missions

The next category has to do with missions. The participants in the study were asked if they had ever served on a mission trip. All of those who answered that they did have the opportunity to serve in missions were either Christian or mature Christians. Interestingly, 0% of the other groups had ever served on a mission trip. It's important to note that this category can be affected by variables like funds, time, etc. That is understandable. However, I have had the opportunity to serve on missions. It wasn't that I was already mature so I went on a mission trip. It was the mission that ushered me into maturity because it expanded my understanding of the kingdom of God, drew my heart to his people, and really changed me forever.

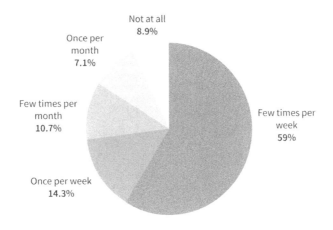

The statistics above are the answers given in general by all participants who labeled themselves as either 'baby Christians', 'struggling Christians', 'Christians', or 'mature Christians' (Appendix A for more details). When we solely looked at those in the study that labeled themselves as 'mature Christians' and their church attendance habits, here's what was discovered:

Church Attendance

The last question I asked was not included in the Lifeway research. It had to do with church attendance. The question was, "How often did you attend church in the last year?" A striking 83% of mature Christians attend church not just once a week, but rather a few times per week. I asked this question because many people are disconnected from the church. This study showed that struggling Christians do not attend church regularly. So we see a strong connection between attending church and maturity. (To see more detailed statistics see Appendix A). When we attend church we are exposing ourselves to mature believers who are living out their faith. We can learn from them only if we are around them. No, the church isn't perfect. Neither are we. But there are good and Godly people in the church who are modeling Christ-like behavior that we should imitate.

While these stats may bore you, they are significant in helping us gain the tools necessary for spiritual growth. We can look at the examples around us of mature believers and emulate them. We can see that mature believers, in fact, display a greater consistency in all areas of Christian activity. There is no getting around it you've got to put in the work in all of these areas. Doing the work leads to growth. Growth leads to maturity.

Teleios

So, what is maturity? The Greek word used for "mature" in Hebrews 5:14 is *teleios* (τέλειος). Vine's Expository Dictionary defines it as "complete, perfect" and states the word *teleios* has its root word in *telos,* meaning "an end or of full age". It has a descriptive aspect to it. If there is an end, then there is a beginning. Maturity not only describes an end but implies that there is a beginning, a starting place. Thus, maturity describes a development, process, or journey. The person on the journey is going through the necessary stages to reach the end goal of maturity. It is a journey in which the person is developing in judgment and wisdom. On this journey, the person is training to have the skill to recognize the difference between right and wrong. Having a discernment between right and wrong will lead to better decision-making that is founded upon the Bible.

In Christianity, we are maturing. When we refer to the idea of *maturing*, we are speaking of a spiritual development that a believer goes through. We are growing into a place where God is in control of everything in our lives, especially the areas that are out of control. Notice the use of the present tense of the verb *maturing*. Maturing conveys growth. It is not instantaneous. We are always, or rather, *should* always be growing in the Lord. It is God's desire to see His church grow into what

God has destined for each one of them. There is an expected development (or journey) of spiritual growth in every Christian from the moment they give their life to Jesus to the moment they pass on to eternity or Jesus returns.

When I was fifteen years old, I was swiftly put into a ministry position out of a great need within the church. The current worship team had decided to move out of town. Yes, the whole worship team. The team consisted of a family of four. The mom sang. The dad played guitar. One son played the drums; the other played the bass. For a while, the church was led with old school tracks playing on a cassette tape in the background. The gap paved the way for me to enter the ministry. While I am extremely grateful for the opportunity, I can definitely say that I was not mature enough to handle some aspects of ministry. Fortunately for me, I had some wonderful leaders to help me navigate those early years. What they taught me is invaluable.

Too often, we skip over stages of spiritual maturity, yet we step into roles of ministry or leadership anyway. If maturity is in fact a journey, then the only way to lead others is if we have journeyed ourselves. It is only when we reach a place of maturity that we can expect to show others the path. Many lists have been created to describe the attributes and qualities of a mature Christian. These lists cover a lot of ground because the topic of maturity is complex. However, there are a few indicators that come straight from the Word of God. Not only can we learn from our own journey, but most importantly, when we search the Scriptures, we can see a biblical format for spiritual development that leads to maturity.

Spiritual Development
Begins with God as the Source

The source of our spiritual development is always God. Philippians 1:6 (NLT) says, *"And I am certain that God, who began the good work within you, will continue his work until it is finally finished on the day when Christ Jesus returns."* It is God who begins any and every good work in us. And it is God who continues that work in us. He is the source. We must acknowledge that we cannot do this on our own. We need to rely on God every day. More to the point, God is the source of everything. He is the source of life. *"Yet for us there is but one God, the Father, who is the source of all things, and we exist for Him; and one Lord, Jesus Christ, by whom are all things [that have been created], and we [believers exist and have life and have been redeemed] through Him"* (1 Corinthians 1:8 AMP). When we maintain a perspective that God is the source of our wake-ups every morning, our security everywhere we travel, the provisions of our work, and everything good that reaches our lives, we build upon our spiritual development. The Scripture clarifies to us, *"for in Him we live and move and have our being"* (Acts 17:28). It is a mistake to take our eyes off the Provisioner of everything, the Creator of who we are, the Maker of heaven and earth. Mature Christians continue to acknowledge that all they had, have, and will continue to have comes from the Father. Furthermore, mature Christians rely on God as the source for their spiritual development. The source is the point of origin. This implies that our spiritual development does not exist without God; in fact, it begins with Him.

So this begs the question... Is God your everything? Until you come to a recognition that He is your everything, a lot of other stuff will take first place in your life. Whatever is in first place will be the driving point of your life.

By the time I turned eighteen, I had a plan for my life. Sure, I was in ministry, but I had a plan set to change the world. I was going to shatter glass ceilings. I enrolled in college and proudly stated my major as pre-law. After all, I had been telling anyone that would listen since I was ten that I was going to be a lawyer or a judge or maybe work for the FBI. I knew what I wanted. Just a few years into my collegiate experience, I felt a relentless tugging from the Holy Spirit drawing me into ministry. At this point, at the age of twenty, God had been working in my life. I began to surrender myself to His will. I didn't become the next Supreme Court Justice, but the benefits of putting God first in my life have given me so much more than I could ever imagine.

Spiritual Development
Continues with Jesus as the Foundation

Mature Christians not only recognize God as the source, but they also search out ways to build up their faith. The first step in the building process is the formation of a solid foundation. The Scriptures teach that we build our faith by building on Christ who is the firm "foundation" (1 Cor. 3:11). In Colossians 2:6-7 (NLT) Paul says, *"And now, just as you accepted Christ Jesus as your Lord, you must continue to follow him. Let your roots grow down into him, and let your lives be built on him. Then your faith will grow strong in the truth you were taught, and you will overflow with thankfulness."* When we accept Jesus as our Lord and Savior, there is an expectation that we continue to follow Jesus. Here, Paul elaborates on what it means to "continue to follow him." First, he speaks about roots. We know that roots are the parts of a flower, plant, or tree that grow down into the earth and provide support. Likewise, we are to grow down into Jesus. We will discuss this later in the text. Next, Paul uses the phrase, "*let your lives be built on him.*"[5] According to Thayer's Greek Lexicon, the word "built" here is defined as: "to finish the structure of which the foundation has already been laid". If we are going to develop, we must build upon the foundation, which is Jesus.

As a young child, I heard a song called "The Wise Man Built His House/Sandyland" by Maranatha Music that never left my heart. You may or may not know it, but nevertheless, the lyrics are embedded in my memory:

> Don't build your house on the sandyland,
> don't build it too near the shore.
> Well, it might be kind of nice, but you'll
> have to build it twice,
> Oh, you'll have to build your house once more
> You better build your house upon a rock.
> Make a good foundation on a solid spot.
> Oh, the storms may come and go, but
> the peace of God you will know.

Mature Christians became mature because they took responsibility for their spiritual development by building into their spiritual lives in meaningful ways. Jesus says it even better:

> *Anyone who listens to my teaching and follows it is wise, like a person who builds a house on solid rock. Though the rain comes in torrents and the floodwaters rise and the winds*

---

5   Colossians 2:7 New Living Translation.

> *beat against that house, it won't collapse because it is built on bedrock. But anyone who hears my teaching and doesn't obey it is foolish, like a person who builds a house on sand. When the rains and floods come and the winds beat against that house, it will collapse with a mighty crash. (Matthew 7:24-27 NLT)*

Jesus clarifies what it means to build the right way. If we listen to His teachings and follow His ways, we are like a person who builds on a solid rock. When the storms of life come, the mature believer will not collapse because they are built on Jesus.

Spiritual development is strengthened through the work of the Holy Spirit in us. Mature believers are mature because they understand that they cannot build on their own. Mature believers understand that they need the help of the Holy Spirit. They build specifically by allowing the Holy Spirit to do His work in them. They always recognize that the Holy Spirit is the one doing the work. Jesus called the Holy Spirit the "advocate" (KJV) or "helper" (NLT) in John 14:16. The original Greek word for "helping" is *paraklētos*. The word is only found five other times in the New Testament and is used four out of the five times to describe the Holy Spirit (the fifth described Jesus). Thayer's Greek Lexicon defines *paraklētos*, "in the widest sense, a helper, succorer, aider, assistant; so of the Holy Spirit destined to take the place of Christ with the apostles (after his ascension to the Father), to lead them to a deeper knowledge of gospel truth, and to give them the divine strength needed to enable them to undergo trials and persecutions on behalf of the divine kingdom." Jesus promised to send the Holy Spirit after He would ascend, so that we would not have to do this journey here on earth alone. Jesus therefore said, "*it is to your advantage that I go away; for if I do not go away, the Helper (Comforter, Advocate,*

Intercessor—Counselor, Strengthener, Standby) will not come to you" (John 16:7 AMP). But it wouldn't be until Jesus left that the Holy Spirit would be given (John 7:39).

In the book of Acts, we see the fulfillment of this promise.[6] The Holy Spirit fell upon those in the upper room and filled them. The Holy Spirit "dwells in us"[7]. If we further consider the complete book of Acts, we see the Holy Spirit's transformational work in the first church, equipping them with power, boldness, and wisdom. As a first example, we can look at the life of Peter. Just prior to the indwelling of the Holy Spirit, Peter was quick-tempered and lacked courage. When the Holy Spirit came down over Peter in Acts 2, a major transformation occurred. The Peter who had cut off the ear of Malchus in the Garden of Gethsemane[8] was now a different man in control of his shaky nature through the power of the Holy Spirit. The Peter who had run in fear and denied knowing Jesus just a few weeks earlier was now the man we see speaking with boldness to a multitude of people.[9] We see an acceleration of maturity in Peter solely through the Holy Spirit.

We can see the same pattern of transformation through the Holy Spirit in other areas of the book of Acts. In Acts 8, we come across a man named Saul who was a great persecutor of the church. *"But Saul was going everywhere to destroy the church. He went from house to house, dragging out both men and women to throw them into prison"* (Acts 8:3 NLT). However, just one chapter later, we see how Saul goes through a transformation, impossible by human standards, yet not impossible through the work of the Holy Spirit (Acts 9:17 NLT).

---

6   Acts 1:8; 2:1-4 New Living Translation.

7   1 Corinthians 3:16 New International Version.

8   John 18:10 New Living Translation.

9   Acts 2:14-39 New Living Translation.

The writer of the book of Acts describes this transformation as "immediate" (Acts 9:20 NLT).

> Maturity is all about being transformed by the Holy Spirit in our mind, soul, and spirit. It is about thinking differently, acting differently, and responding to the Father differently.

Paul describes this transformation as a veil that has been taken away and is now changing us into the image of God. *"So all of us who have had that veil removed can see and reflect the glory of the Lord. And the Lord—who is the Spirit—makes us more and more like him as we are changed into his glorious image"* (2 Cor. 3:18 NLT).

The same Holy Spirit that worked in Paul, Peter, and the first church is still here, alive and active. He dwells in every believer and is available to help them grow into maturity. That is good news. That means that the Holy Spirit will also work in you if you let Him. The transformation that we go through is evidence that we have surrendered our lives to God. Just as I was confronted many years ago to surrender my plans to God, you will be, too.

In the next chapter, we will explore how the Holy Spirit accelerates transformation in our lives to help us reach a life of maturity in our mind, soul, and spirit.

CHAPTER THREE

SEEDS AND ROOTS

Ж

I tell you the truth, unless a kernel of wheat is
planted in the soil and dies, it remains alone.
But its death will produce many new kernels—
a plentiful harvest of new lives.

John 12:24 NLT

In the previous chapters, we learned that, as believers, we are expected to grow (1 Cor. 3:11). This growth is a process that takes us into a spiritual maturity. We also learned that spiritual maturity is a journey, and that journey has a beginning and an end.

In our human development, we are born, and then we die. In our spiritual development, we die to self and thus are born into new life. It is a statement that goes against the human intellect, and rightly so, because it is beyond the natural. None of this can be accomplished if not for the powerful, transforming work of the Holy Spirit in our lives.

A few years ago, we were looking for a new home, and I quickly began petitioning the Lord for a gardening space. I am so grateful that the house He gave me has a garden bed and lots of fruit trees and bushes. I love the process of planting and harvesting. It is so satisfying to plant a seed and see the results. Getting to eat from the fruit of your labor is also a great benefit. Since living here, I have found that planting and harvesting has taught me so many valuable lessons and connections to the Word of God.

The Death of a Seed

As I studied what a seed is, I learned that most seeds are covered by an outer layer called the seed coat. That seed coat must break down to begin the growing process. Jesus describes it as dying.

In John 12:24, Jesus uses the illustration of a seed to depict the process of maturity. Of course, Jesus is speaking of his impending sacrifice on the cross in this verse, but nevertheless, we can see an inevitable law of nature commanded by God in this passage: only through the death of a seed can fruit be produced. He begins with an "I tell you the truth" statement. In other words, there is no other way. There is only one way in the spiritual; death is what produces life. The death Jesus is speaking of is not a physical one. It is a spiritual death. When we die to our old self (the self before coming to know Jesus), we start the growing process.

> *We know that our old sinful selves were crucified with Christ so that sin might lose its power in our lives. We are no longer*

*slaves to sin. For when we died with Christ we were set free
from the power of sin. And since we died with Christ, we
know we will also live with him (Romans 6:6-8 NLT)*

We are that Seed

On another occasion, Jesus uses a parable about seeds to explain
the kingdom of heaven. In Matthew 13:24 (NIV), He says that
the "kingdom of heaven is like a man who sowed good seed in
his field." Now, there is much more to this parable than just
the aforementioned. This parable is about planting good seeds.
Let's look at the verse in its context:

> Here is another story Jesus told: *"The Kingdom of Heav-
> en is like a farmer who planted good seed in his field. But
> that night as the workers slept, his enemy came and planted
> weeds among the wheat, then slipped away. When the crop
> began to grow and produce grain, the weeds also grew. The
> farmer's workers went to him and said, 'Sir, the field where
> you planted that good seed is full of weeds! Where did they
> come from?' 'An enemy has done this!' the farmer exclaimed.
> 'Should we pull out the weeds?' they asked. 'No,' he replied,
> 'you'll uproot the wheat if you do. Let both grow together
> until the harvest. Then I will tell the harvesters to sort out
> the weeds, tie them into bundles, and burn them, and to put
> the wheat in the barn'" (Matthew 13:24-30 NIV).*

Some parables in the scriptures have no explanation. However,
this one does. Jesus explains the parable at length in the same
chapter, just a few verses later.[10] Let's break down this parable
and see how it helps us understand the concept of the seed.

---

10   Matthew 13:36-43 New Living Translation.

The Kingdom of Heaven

To understand this parable, we first need to know that Jesus is talking about planting spiritual seeds. How do we know this? Because Jesus opens this parable with the phrase "the kingdom of heaven" (verse 24). This phrase is found throughout the New Testament. It is most notably in reference to our inward state as both John the Baptist and Jesus use it to refer to repentance (Matt. 3:2; 4:7 NLT). It is also used in the Beatitudes and in parables that describe what heaven is like. Before we even begin to think about planting seeds in our life, we must first understand that there is a battle for our soul. The battle for our soul is between the kingdom of heaven and the kingdom of darkness. Jesus starts with the phrase "the kingdom of heaven" to show the contrast between where all good exists (the kingdom of heaven) versus where sin exists (the kingdom of darkness).

A Farmer

There is a man here who is planting (verse 24). Later, in verse 27, this man is referred to as the "owner". If the kingdom of heaven is like a man planting seeds, then this man is not just any man, but rather Jesus himself sowing good seeds into this world. Jesus came to sow the greatest seed in our life, the seed of salvation. Later, in Matthew 13:37, Jesus explains the parable and refers to the farmer as the "son of man", or himself.

The Field

The field is where the seed is planted. The field is no mystery, as Jesus goes on to explain in verse 38. The field here is "the world". The world is a place where the seeds are planted.

The Seeds

In this parable, the good seed is distinguishable from the bad seed. The farmer planted good seeds, but while the workers were sleeping, the enemy came and planted bad seeds. The good seeds produced wheat, a valuable source of sustenance. The bad seeds produced tares, a useless substance. Tares are weeds. Weeds have no purpose. They are a nuisance. They exist to steal the nutrients that the good seeds need. Jesus goes on to explain in verse 38 that the good seeds are the "sons of the kingdom", and the bad seeds are the "sons of the wicked one".

Jesus has come to change our lives. He planted a good seed in us. He planted the seed of salvation in our hearts. This seed has the power to produce life in us, but we must die to our old selves. We must cultivate the good seed in our lives, while at the same time, uproot the bad seed.

The Enemy Plants Seeds

The scripture has a great deal to say about seeds. One of the areas that we are warned about is the seeds that the enemy plants. We can clearly see in the parable of Matthew 13 that there are good seeds, and there are bad seeds. Just as Jesus came to plant a good seed in our hearts, the enemy will always come into our lives with a bad seed that produces something of no value. This seed is planted to choke up the good seed that was planted. And, if successful, the bad seed will ruin our good seed. The enemy is always trying to stunt our spiritual growth; he is always trying to stop our maturity. If he can't stop you from being saved, he will try to stop you from growing stronger in the Lord by planting bad seeds all around you. The enemy is astute. He is hoping that the good seed that Jesus plants in your heart will not take root and that the bad seed he plants does.

Roots

And now, just as you accepted Christ Jesus as your Lord, you must continue to follow him. Let your roots grow down into him, and let your lives be built on him. Then your faith will grow strong in the truth you were taught, and you will overflow with thankfulness

Colossians 2:6-7 NLT

After the seed dies, it begins to sprout. The small bud of a seed is what you see on the surface, but in the ground, the seed has begun to take root. In fact, what you see above ground is not nearly as important as what is beneath it. Despite rarely being exposed, roots are an extremely important part of the plant or tree. As a matter of fact, roots make up about fifty percent of the tree. Earlier, we mentioned that we are the seed. If we are the seed as Jesus stated in Matthew 13, then the roots are the unseen parts of who we are.

Growing roots is referred to as being "rooted" by the scriptures. Strong's Exhaustive Concordance states the word *rhizoo* (root) in Colossians is defined as "to cause to strike root", "to strengthen with roots", "to render firm", or "to cause a person or thing to be firmly grounded". Paul is telling the Colossians here to be rooted in Christ. To grow their roots in Jesus. To be firmly grounded in the Savior.

As stated earlier, roots are the unseen parts of who we are. The Bible describes those unseen parts of who we are as the "inner" being or "inward" man. In Romans 7:22 (NIV), Paul says, "For in my inner being I delight in God's law." Larry Pierce, the author of the online Bible, outlines the biblical usage of "inner being" as the internal inner man or the soul.[11] The Bible further describes us as being made up of three parts: spirit, soul, and body (1 Thes. 5:23 NIV).

Spirit

Our spirit is our innermost man. Strong's Exhaustive Concordance specifies that the original Greek word here for spirit is *pneuma*. This is the same word that partially describes the Holy Spirit, *hagios pnuema*. This allows us to see that there is a connection between our spirit and the Holy Spirit. The connections we make with God are done in our spirit. The scripture says that *"God is spirit, and his worshipers must worship in the Spirit and in truth"* (John 4:24 NIV). Our spirit is the part of us that is aware of God. It connects with the Holy Spirit of God through Jesus. Our spirit is guided by the Holy Spirit and fed by the Word of God.

Soul

Our soul is our heart, mind, will, and emotions. It is where our feelings, desires, and affections exist. Strong's Exhaustive Concordance says that the original Greek word here for soul is *psyche*. This is the same word that is used in Hebrews 4:12 (NLT), *"For the word of God is alive and powerful. It is sharper than the sharpest two-edged sword, cutting between soul and spirit, between joint and marrow. It exposes our innermost thoughts and*

---

11   Blue Letter Bible, "G2080 - esō - Strong's Greek Lexicon (kjv)," November 30, 2021. https://www.blueletterbible.org/lexicon/g2080/kjv/tr/0-1/

desires." There is a clear biblical division between our spirit and our soul. Our soul is the part that is aware of ourselves. It is the "me" of who we are. Our soul is fed by our choices. We will revisit this idea a bit later.

Body

Our body is the physical container for our soul and spirit, sometimes referred to as the "flesh" in scripture. And Strong's Exhaustive Concordance explains that the original Greek word for body is *soma*. It is the part of man that experiences the world—the part that is aware of the world through the senses: sight, sound, smell, taste, and touch.

Let's take another glance at 1 Thessalonians 5:23 (NLT), "*Now may the God of peace make you holy in every way, and may your whole spirit and soul and body be kept blameless until our Lord Jesus Christ comes again.*" All of who we are—spirit, soul, and body—need to be found blameless.

We live in a world that offers us sinful pleasures, forced inappropriate experiences, and stressors. Peter says that every day they "*wage war against your very soul*" (1 Peter 2:11 NLT). We are part of a world that is broken and sinful. There is a real enemy that is vying for your soul. The body desires worldly pleasure, and the spirit desires connection with the Father. Each is pulling for your soul.

> The condition of your soul is determined by what is being fed the most—the body or the spirit.

If you are feeding your body with the sinful pleasures of the world, your soul will be controlled by sin. If you are feeding your spirit with the Word of God, your soul will be controlled by the spirit.

Illustration 1. Spirit, Soul, and Body

Illustration 1 provides a visual of how the choices we make affect our soul.[12] The believer who is led by the Holy Spirit is more inclined to make a choice in the spirit man; thus, the soul is controlled by the spirit. An individual who is led by the flesh will make a choice in the body or physical man. Thus, the soul is controlled by the flesh. Romans 8:5 says, "*Those who live according to the flesh have their minds set on what the flesh desires; but those who live in accordance with the Spirit have their minds set on what the Spirit desires.*"

When we come to know Jesus, the Holy Spirit makes a home in our heart. He becomes our guide. Jesus said that when the Holy Spirit would come, "*He will guide you*" (John 16:13 NLT). The Holy Spirit helps us make the right choices.

---

12   Created by author.

Our soul is what needs saving. This is why we need Jesus to plant that seed of salvation deep in our soul. James says that we need to "*humbly accept the word God has planted in your hearts because it has the power to save your soul*" (James 1:21 NLT). Our soul needs a savior. Our soul cannot function appropriately without the control of the Holy Spirit. It can run wild. It can grow stronger than the spirit.

There is a hierarchy when it comes to the spirit, soul, body. First Thessalonians 5:23 places the three-part man in order. The believer is to be controlled by the spirit. Then the spirit can control the soul, particularly when the soul is looking to take part in sinful, negligent, or dangerous behavior. Then the body can honor God. In turn, we can present our whole self—spirit, soul, and body—blameless before the Lord. Whichever part you feed will grow. We need to feed the spirit. Feeding the spirit is only done through connection with God.

We feed our spirit with the Word of God. Jesus said that "man shall not live on bread alone, but on every word that comes from the mouth of God" (Matthew 4:4 NIV). All maturity must rely on feeding the spirit. The Word of God provides "milk" (1 Peter 2:2 NLT). The Word of God is "meat" (1 Corinthians 3:2 NLT).

We also feed our spirit with Jesus. Multiple times, Jesus said He is the "bread of life" (John 6:33). In John 4:32 (NIV), Jesus told the disciples, "*I have food to eat that you know nothing about.*"

Lastly, *we feed our spirit by doing the will of God.* Jesus continues to speak of this spiritual food in John 4:34. He says, "my food is to do the will of Him who sent me, and to finish His work."[13]

---

13   John 4:34 New International Version.

Healthy vs Unhealthy Roots

As we feed our spirit, we are growing our roots deep down into Jesus. Healthy roots grow in our soul as we feed the spirit. Unhealthy roots grow in our soul as we feed the flesh. As in life, there are healthy things and unhealthy things. Roots play a significant role in the health of a tree. There are characteristics of healthy trees, and one of those characteristics lies beneath the ground in healthy roots. A healthy tree has roots that absorb, channel, store, and anchor.[14]

Absorb. A healthy tree starts with roots that absorb water, minerals, and nutrients. Without these components, the leaves of the tree wither, the branches crack, and fruit cannot be produced. Just as a tree has roots that absorb water, minerals, and nutrients, our life must absorb these important things into the roots of our soul.

The water is representative of the Word of God. We need to fill our lives with the Word of God to strengthen our roots "deep down" into Jesus. Jesus gave up His life in order that we might be "holy and clean, washed by the cleansing of God's word" (Eph. 5:26 NLT). As we absorb God's word into our lives, we are transformed. The key is to stop the absorption of foreign substances into the soul.

---

14   J.M. Sillick and W.R. Jacobi, "Healthy Roots and Healthy Trees - 2.926," Extension (Colorado State University, September 16, 2019), https://extension. colostate.edu/topic-areas/yard-garden/healthy-roots-and-healthy-trees-2-926/

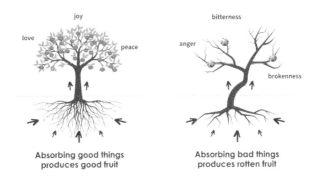

Absorbing good things
produces good fruit

Absorbing bad things
produces rotten fruit

Illustration 2. Healthy vs Unhealthy Roots

Illustration 2 gives a visual of how what we absorb into our roots will affect what grows.[15] Think of the roots as our soul. Think of the things we absorb as what the spirit offers (good things) or what the flesh offers (bad things). Whatever it is we absorb makes a home in our souls and channels up into our being to produce either good fruit or rotten fruit.

What have you absorbed in your roots over the course of your life? All our experiences in life can easily be absorbed into our inner man. If the experiences are positive, they most likely will set a course for the growth of "good fruit". If the experiences are negative, they could potentially set up a course for the growth of "rotten fruit". Uprooting the negative issues of life is complicated. That's why the Word of God is essential as the "water" we absorb cleanses out the negative issues that have taken root in our hearts. We need to absorb the Word of God because the word replaces our negative experiences with new information and perspective.

---

15   Created by author.

Water isn't the only thing absorbed in our roots. Healthy trees absorb minerals and nutrients that come from the soil content. The soil is essential in the feeding of the roots. Where a tree is planted makes all the difference in its survival. Where you are planted makes a difference in your survival. Jesus told a parable about seeds being planted in Matthew 13:1-23. Where the seeds were planted determined the fate of the plant. Some seed was planted on a "path". The birds came along and ate the seed. Some seed was planted on rocky places. The seed grew quickly, but because it did not have much soil, it did not have deep roots. Therefore, the sun scorched it, and it withered and died. The next seed fell among thorns. As the seed grew into plants, so did the thorns, and the thorns eventually choked the good plants. However, other seeds did fall on good soil. They grew up to produce a crop. From this parable, we can see that where we are planted makes a difference in our spiritual growth.

We need to absorb the correct nutrients and minerals that come from where we are planted. It is imperative to be planted in good soil. First and foremost, we need to be planted in Jesus. But we also should look for ways that help us stay planted in Jesus. According to Hawkins and Clinton, authors of *The New Christian Counselor*, these ways include resources such as counseling or therapy, a church community, and a support system of friends and family.

Channel. A healthy tree starts with roots that absorb water, minerals, and nutrients and channels it up into its leaves and fruit like a conduit. The fruit is only as good as its roots. Healthy roots will produce healthy fruit. And healthy fruit gives way to more seeds. As stated earlier and seen in illustration 2, the root system of a tree is similar to our soul. If we absorb spiritual things in our soul, we will produce spiritual things. If we absorb the flesh, we will produce the flesh. What we absorb in our inner man is what we will produce in our outer man.

> *No good tree bears bad fruit, nor does a bad tree bear good fruit. Each tree is recognized by its own fruit. People do not pick figs from thornbushes, or grapes from briers. A good man brings good things out of the good stored up in his heart, and an evil man brings evil things out of the evil stored up in his heart. For the mouth speaks what the heart is full of (Luke 6:43-45 NIV).*

The idea of good producing good and bad producing bad is a biblical principle. There is no other way around it. This is a concept that is imperative to understand. Your strong inner man will produce a strong outer man. According to Strong's Exhaustive Concordance, the word "heart" here is *kardia,* and its biblical usage is not only "the heart", but also the "thoughts or feelings". In other words, what we absorb in our inner man (heart, thoughts, and feelings) can affect our outer man (physical being and circumstances). As a tree channels up what it takes in through its roots, so must we to remain strong in the Lord. A tree absorbs and channels daily. We need to absorb good things daily.

Much of what we absorb starts in our mind. We cannot control everything that is done to us, but we can control a lot of what is absorbed. There are moments where experiences are forced on us. However, there are moments where we dive into experiences at our own volition. James puts it this way: "*Temptation comes from our own desires, which entice us and drag us away. These desires give birth to sinful actions. And when sin is allowed to grow, it gives birth to death*" (James 1:14-15 NLT). The temptation starts with a desire, the feeling that we need it (the enticing part). We continue to think about that desire (the part where we allow it to grow). That desire drops into our heart and eventually becomes an action (sin) and consequently leads to death (separation from the Lord).

This is why the scripture says that we should *"take captive every thought to make it obedient to Christ"* (2 Cor. 10:5 NIV). When the thought comes into our mind, we have a choice (see Illustration 1). We can either feed that thought or stop it by taking it to Jesus. Choose to take the thought captive by surrendering it to Jesus. Understand that you cannot control many things and that God is the one in control. As you do that, you begin to shift perspectives, and shifting perspectives shifts what we absorb.

Dr. Michelle Pierce, a psychologist, talks about the effects of thinking on the brain, body, and behavior. In her book, *Cognitive Behavior Therapy for Christians with Depression*, she states that the more we have a particular thought, the stronger that thought becomes; the less we have that thought, the weaker it becomes. It sounds simple enough, but it's true.

One final point she makes is this, "Our mental activity also influences what emotions we feel and how intensely we feel them." In other words, as we continue to preoccupy ourselves with the thoughts, our emotions are making stronger connections with those thoughts. The emotions and thoughts strongly connect and we soon find ourselves making moves with a force that at times can be like a runaway train on its way to an inevitable crash.

We talked about thoughts. If we can take hold of the negative thought and take it captive to Jesus, then we can stop the negative consequences from coming to fruition. But what happens when the thought does drop into our heart? What do we do then? With God's help, we can learn how to take thoughts captive, to replace thoughts with better things (Phil. 4:8), and to also lean into the fruit of the Spirit for our greater transformation.

CHAPTER FOUR

FRUIT

Therefore by their fruit you will know them.

Matthew 7:20 NIV

We have been talking about the process of growth: growing out of infancy and growing into maturity. The Bible uses an incredible number of examples that compare our life of growth to nature, specifically trees, and almost all of these examples lead to the final purpose of maturity. Remember that the original word for maturity is *teleios*, as stated in Vine's Expository Dictionary. *Teleios* describes a journey, and the person on the journey is going through the necessary stages to reach the end goal of maturity—adulthood. Adulthood is a place where a person has developed judgment and wisdom.

> In Christianity, we are maturing. We are growing into
> a place where God is so in control that what grows
> in our lives are godly things.

Jesus said, *"Therefore by their fruits you will know them,"* (Matt.
7:20 NIV). By our fruit, we will be known. Let's look at this
passage in its context:

> *By their fruit you will recognize them. Do people pick grapes
> from thornbushes, or figs from thistles? Likewise, every good
> tree bears good fruit, but a bad tree bears bad fruit. A good
> tree cannot bear bad fruit, and a bad tree cannot bear good
> fruit. Every tree that does not bear good fruit is cut down and
> thrown into the fire. Thus, by their fruit you will recognize
> them (Matthew 7:16-20 NIV).*

The passage in full detail says that some people are recognized
by their fruit. As a matter of fact, it must be really important
because Jesus says that same phrase twice. It is the very first
thing we read in verse 16 and the very last thing we read in verse
20. It is a simple principle: the fruit you see hanging on the tree
will tell you what kind of tree it is.

I have three cherry trees, a peach tree, a fig tree, and two pear
trees on my property. When we first moved in, I did not know
what kind of trees these were. After the summer passed, I clearly
understood what type of trees they were because their fruit
defined them.

Jesus poses a question in the passage. In verse 16, He asks, *"Do
people pick grapes from thornbushes, or figs from thistles?"* The

reality is that we cannot expect apples from an orange tree or bananas from an apple tree. Every tree will bear fruit from the seed it is from.

A bad tree will bear bad fruit; a good tree will bear good fruit. Notice that the fruit comes from the root. Jesus said the tree will bear or produce the fruit. This means that what we plant in our lives grows into a tree, and that tree will produce the kind of fruit that it was originally intended to produce. In other words, you cannot expect to produce fruit you did not plant. So, this begs the question: What have you planted? Because according to Jesus, "*every tree that does not bear good fruit is cut down and thrown into the fire*" (Matt. 7:19 NIV). There is no other use for a tree that does not bear fruit.

The word "fruit", or its relatives "fruitful" and "fruits", are found upwards of about sixty-seven times in fifty-eight verses in the New Testament.[16] Forty-one of these times it is used figuratively as an expression of what is happening in the person's spirit. Like a tree displays fruit, a person's spirit displays character.

Perhaps one of the most famous passages about fruit is found in Galatians 5:22-23 (NLT), "*But the Holy Spirit produces this kind of fruit in our lives: love, joy, peace, patience, kindness, goodness, faithfulness, gentleness, and self-control. There is no law against these things!*" The word "fruit" here is translated from the Greek word *karpos*. Strong's Exhaustive Concordance explains that *karpos* means "that which originates from something, an effect, result".

---

16   "KJV Search Results for "fruit"." Blue Letter Bible. Accessed 23 Dec, 2021. https://www.blueletterbible.org//search/search.cfm?Criteria=fruit&t=K-JV#s=s_primary_0_1

That which originates from something is the effect of something. It is the result of something. Vine's Expository Dictionary defines "fruit" metaphorically as being the "visible expression of power working inwardly and invisibly, the character of the "fruit" being evidence of the character of the power producing it. As the visible expressions of hidden lusts are the works of the flesh, so the invisible power of the Holy Spirit in those who are brought into living union with Christ produces "the fruit of the Spirit,"."

Visible Expression. Fruit is a visible expression. Not much of who we are can be seen, but what is seen of who we are should reflect what comes from the inside. What we are inside will reflect on the outside. We need to make sure that what is reflected is good fruit.

Power Working Inwardly. Jesus said that "*every good tree produces good fruit*," (Matt. 7:17 NIV). The key here is that something inwardly is working in us, specifically a power working in us. The power working in us comes from the person of the Holy Spirit. In Acts 1:8 (NLT), Jesus promised that we would receive "power when the Holy Spirit comes on [us]." There is a power working inwardly in us to produce good fruit. That power is not just an emotion, innate, or natural. This power comes from the Holy Spirit, and it is supernatural. Jesus promised us that, when He would leave, He would not leave us alone. He said that the third person of the Trinity would come to be with us so that we would not be alone. In John 14:16-18, Jesus promised us the Holy Spirit.

And I will ask the Father, and he will give you another advocate to help you and be with you forever— the Spirit of truth. The world cannot accept him, because it neither sees him nor knows him. But you know him, for he lives with you and will be in you. I will not leave you as orphans; I will come to you (John 14:16-18 NIV).

Jesus said that the person of the Holy Spirit will be "with you" and "in you". He is the power working inwardly in us. It is the Holy Spirit in us that is working good fruit. The Holy Spirit is given to us on the day we accept Jesus. He is the third person of the Trinity. God is the Creator. Jesus is the Savior. And the Holy Spirit acts on behalf of God's will for this world and for our lives by helping us, comforting us, counseling us, guiding us, and empowering us. He has the power to actively work in our lives, and He has the power to produce the good fruit that Jesus talks about.

This inward working is similar to what is shown in Illustration 2. The inward man is being worked on by the power of the Holy Spirit. As the Spirit works good things in our hearts and minds (roots), we begin to produce godly things in our lives (fruit).

Power Working Invisibly. The Holy Spirit works inwardly and invisibly. While we cannot see Him, we can most definitely see His work. The greatest evidence of the work of the Holy Spirit is what we see in ourselves. We know who we are inwardly, and we know the change the Holy Spirit has produced in us. This invisible work is much like wind. We are not saying that the Holy Spirit is wind, nor are we diminishing the work of the Holy Spirit by equating Him to wind. However, the scriptures use the example of "wind" in Acts 2:2 (NIV), so that we understand the work of the Holy Spirit. We use the analogy because you cannot see the wind, but you can feel it. You cannot see the wind, but there is evidence in the rustling of the trees, the flowing movement of the tall grass, or the breeze in your face that the wind is blowing. Jesus said in John 3:8 (NIV), *"The wind blows where it wishes. You hear its sound, but you do not know where it comes from or where it is going. So it is with everyone born of the Spirit."*

Character of the fruit being evidence of the character of the power producing it. What a powerful statement we find in Vine's Expository Dictionary. It is imperative for us to understand the role of the Holy Spirit in our life. We will discuss this in further detail; however, for the sake of this point, it is essential that we understand that, as we let the Holy Spirit do His work in us, we will produce evidence of His work in us. That evidence is called FRUIT of the Spirit.

Fruit is not something that is developed on its own. There is something that produces the fruit. For us Christians, it is the Holy Spirit. As stated earlier, the greatest scriptural passage on this topic can be found in Galatians 5:22-23 (NIV), *"But the fruit of the Spirit is love, joy, peace, forbearance, kindness, goodness, faithfulness, gentleness and self-control. Against such things there is no law."*

It is no coincidence that Paul uses fruit to help us understand the work of the Holy Spirit in us. Fruit is sweet, and everything that God does in our lives is also sweet. Paul gives us quite the list of fruit produced by the Holy Spirit. He tells us that the fruit is a direct result (effect) of the Holy Spirit (originator) working in us. It is not the result of my spirit or my power, but the result of the Holy Spirit working in me.

The Fruits of the Spirit are not Emotions

We ascribe love, joy, peace, and patience to emotions, so it's no wonder we often think of the fruit of the Spirit as feelings and emotions. One thing we must understand is that, although the fruit of the Spirit seem to be emotional in context, they are not emotions. Emotions are natural; they are part of our humanity. The fruit of the Spirit are supernatural, and they come from the supernatural.

Emotions are natural. Human emotions are primarily produced based on our circumstances. What is happening around us tends to direct our emotions. This is why so many of us fall into depression, anxiety, fear, chaos, etc. If we could handle our emotions on our own naturally, there would be no need for the fruit of the Holy Spirit. However, we cannot do it on our own. Humanity has proven this throughout history.

Emotions are God-given. They are a gift from God. He wants us to feel what love, joy, peace, etc., are. Unfortunately, sin entered this world, and the enemy uses our flesh and circumstances to provoke unhealthy displays of emotions. In fact, we are made in the image of God. He has emotions. In his book *Anatomy of the Soul*, Dr. Curt Thompson takes a look at Genesis 6:6 and suggests that it describes God's emotional experience:

> The Lord regretted that he had made human beings on the earth, and his heart was deeply troubled. (Genesis 6:6:) This is one of the most poignant sentences in all of Scripture. Not only does it describe God's emotional experience, it connects his emotional response directly to humankind.

Feelings and emotions are not bad, but God knows that man has a hard time balancing his emotions, so He sent His only Son to demonstrate all the fruit of the Spirit here on earth. And when Jesus connected us back to God through His death and resurrection, the Holy Spirit stepped in to help us achieve the example of Jesus.

As individuals, emotions can rule us. When circumstances around us shift, our emotions can run high. If we are not guided by the Holy Spirit, we tend to move naturally and instinctively from our own state of mind. Our hearts and minds are the holding ground for our emotions. Proverbs 4:23 (NIV) says, *"Above all else, guard your heart, for it is the wellspring of life."* The NLT version says, *"Guard your heart above all else, for it determines the course of your life."* The heart has a great influence over your life. This is exactly why we need to be led by the Holy Spirit. Emotions are not bad; they just need to be controlled through the Holy Spirit.

I have found myself ruled by my emotions at times. I had to apologize many times for my swift and choleric responses. It was a terrible character flaw that I had to give up to the Lord. Don't get me wrong, I am still far from perfect, but when I realized what the fruit of the Holy Spirit were and how they can help me govern my emotions, it was life-changing for me.

The Fruit of the Spirit are Characteristics, Attributes, and Qualities

The Fruit of the Spirit are characteristics, attributes, and qualities that help us manage our emotions. The Holy Spirit can help us love when it is difficult to love. The Holy Spirit can help us have joy when everything around us is falling apart. The

Holy Spirit can help us to be patient when we are desperate to have an answer.

Allowing the Holy Spirit to pour out His fruit in our life will help us to understand what real love, joy, peace, etc., are and how they function in our lives. So many of us come to Jesus with a tattered past. At times, the past is a consequence of our own actions, and other times, we did nothing to deserve the terrible things that happened to us. Nonetheless, we come to Jesus with a past full of experiences. These past experiences have distorted the real love, joy, and peace that God intended for us to experience in our lives.

The Bible says that Satan is the "*father of lies*" (John 8:44 NIV). Sin, this broken world, and the enemy himself are constantly misrepresenting the very emotions that God has created for us to enjoy life. Since the beginning of humanity, the enemy himself has distorted the truth. In the garden of Eden, he deliberately misled Eve.[17] He continues and will continue in the last days to deceive many.[18]

Scripture says that good fruit will come by way of the Holy Spirit.[19] Bad fruit will come by way of our sinful nature.[20] Paul says that spirit and the flesh are both "*in conflict with each other*" (Galatians 5:17 NIV). There is a sinful nature that is inside of all of us. Paul calls it the flesh. We need the Holy Spirit to connect to our spirit to help influence the flesh. The way we break the sinful nature is by belonging to Christ.[21] Then the Holy Spirit can come in and help us manage the flesh. The Holy Spirit

---

17   Genesis 3:1-7
18   1 Timothy 4:1
19   Galatians 5:22-23 New International Version.
20   Galatians 5:19-21 New International Version.
21   Galatians 5:24 New International Version.

will help us manage our emotions so that we produce good fruit. The Holy Spirit will help us see through the enemy's lies and distortions to help us build up maturity by planting these wonderful characteristics, attributes, and qualities.

The Fruit of the Spirit is a Sign of Maturity

We need the characteristics, attributes, and qualities of the fruit of the Holy Spirit working in us so that we can reach maturity in Christ. A mature tree should bear fruit. It often takes around three to five years for a newly-planted, young tree to actually bear fruit. When it does bear fruit, it is a sign that the tree has reached maturity. Jesus stated this very fundamental truth.

> *I am the true vine, and my Father is the gardener. He cuts off every branch in me that bears no fruit, while every branch that does bear fruit he prunes so that it will be even more fruitful. You are already clean because of the word I have spoken to you. Remain in me, as I also remain in you. No branch can bear fruit by itself; it must remain in the vine. Neither can you bear fruit unless you remain in me.*

> *"I am the vine; you are the branches. If you remain in me and I in you, you will bear much fruit; apart from me you can do nothing. If you do not remain in me, you are like a branch that is thrown away and withers; such branches are picked up, thrown into the fire and burned. If you remain in me and my words remain in you, ask whatever you wish, and it will be done for you. This is to my Father's glory, that you bear much fruit, showing yourselves to be my disciples* (John 15:1-8 NIV).

In this passage of John 15, Jesus uses the phrase of *bear fruit* multiple times, which indicates to us that there is an expectation for every Christian to bear fruit. And an even greater lesson is that of *not* bearing fruit. For Jesus says that *"He [the Father] cuts off every branch in me that bears no fruit"* (John 15:2 NIV). As long as we "remain" in Jesus, the vine, we will bear fruit. That is the expectation.

God is the gardener. Strong's Exhaustive Concordance describes a "gardener" as a tiller of the soil. He is the person who works the soil, cares for the atmosphere, and creates the best environment for the vine to thrive. Paul says it best in 1 Corinthians 3:6 (NIV), *"I planted the seed, Apollos watered it, but God has been making it grow."* God is the one in control of each person's surroundings. God's intentions are for us all to grow.

The concept is that Jesus is the true vine. The vine is that part that sends out the necessary nutrients, but it also supports the rest of the parts of the vine. Jesus is that vine. Strong's Exhaustive Concordance reveals that "Christ calls himself a vine, because, as the vine imparts to its branches sap and productiveness, so Christ infuses into his followers his own divine strength and life." In Him, we are fed and supported. He supports our spiritual walk. This is an important perspective that every Christian needs to know. We must be willing to give our life to Jesus in order to be productive and bear the fruit of the Spirit.

The final ingredient in this recipe of growth of discipleship in John 15 is the branches. Jesus says that we are the branches, and there are three things done to branches. First, any branch that does not bear fruit is cut off. Second, any branch that does not remain in Jesus will be picked up and thrown into the fire.

Third, He prunes the branches that remain in Him, so that they can bear even more fruit. We see three categories of branches, or believers: those that bear no fruit, those that do not remain in Christ, and those that bear fruit and are pruned. The way to turn our life around is to remain in Christ and allow God to work in our life (prune) through the power of the Holy Spirit.

CHAPTER FIVE

THE FRUIT OF THE SPIRIT: INWARD FRUIT

> But the Holy Spirit produces this kind of fruit in our lives: love, joy, peace, patience, kindness, goodness, faithfulness, gentleness, and self-control. There is no law against these things!
>
> Galatians 5:22-23 NLT

In the previous chapter, we introduced the Fruit of the Spirit with three important points. First, the Fruit of the Spirit are not emotions. Second, the Fruit of the Spirit are characteristics, attributes, and qualities that the Holy Spirit plants in us to help us govern our emotions. Third, the Fruit of the Spirit working in our lives is a sign of maturity.

When we look carefully at these nine fruit, we can divide them into three categories. There is fruit that we eat, fruit that we give to others, and fruit that we give back to God. While the scripture does not categorize them this way, I find it helps me understand them better.

Inward Fruit

Inward fruit are the fruit we bear and eat. These are the fruit we need to experience. The three fruits in this category (which we will discuss in detail later on) are love, joy, and peace.

Outward Fruit

Not all the fruit that we bear are meant to be eaten alone. Outward fruit are fruit that we bear yet give to others. The three fruits in this category are patience, kindness, and goodness.

Onward Fruit

We don't just consume and give to others to consume. We also take the seeds that are in our fruit and plant them to make more fruit. That's part of the maturity process, recognizing that what we have comes from our Creator. The way we give back to God is by taking the seed found in the fruit we bear and planting it to produce more for the kingdom. Onward fruit are the fruit that keep us moving forward in the Lord. The three fruits in this category are faithfulness, gentleness, and self-control.

Inward Fruit: Love

The very first fruit listed is love. Why does Paul list the first fruit as love? Because all of Christianity—its entire message—is built on love. John 3:16 (NIV) says, *"For God so loved the world that he gave his one and only Son, that whoever believes in him shall not perish but have eternal life."* God loves the world. That was the reason that He sent Jesus to die on the cross for our sins.

Unfortunately, the English language has many definitions for the word "love". To help us further understand the greater concept of love in the scriptures, we need to break down a few of the most familiar "loves" we experience in life and relate them to the Bible. In his book, *Four Loves*, C.S. Lewis describes four types of loves that we experience in life: affection, friendship, eros, and charity. Today, many refer to the Greek words used, either in scripture or during the first church period, to describe the loves that we are most familiar with.

Storge. One of the first loves we come to experience in life is the love of a parent. While we don't find the word *storge* in the Bible, we do find its concept. *Philostorgos* is found in Romans 12:10 (NLT), *"Love each other with genuine affection, and take delight in honoring each other."* It comes from the root words *philos* and *storge*. Strong's Exhaustive Concordance defines *philostorgos* as cherishing one's kindred, especially parents or children. It is a love that describes parental bonds and family unity. We can see beautiful examples of the exchange of *philostorgos* love in the Bible between Abraham and Isaac.[22]

Philia. Another love we experience in life is that of *philadelphia*, sometimes known as *philia* because of the root word. It is a word

---

we find in the scriptures, and it refers to love that Christians cherish for each other.[23] It is a brotherly love. It is a bond that believers have with each other. It is a bond you may have with a friend. It is a love that unifies. Some say that this is the love that David and Jonathan had for each other.[24]

Eros. One of the first ideas of love that the human brain thinks of is that of love between a man and a woman. In *Four Loves*, C.S. Lewis describes *eros* love as "being in love; or, if you prefer, that kind of love which lovers are in". While we do not find this exact word in the Bible, we find its concept. *Eros* is a romantic love. It is appropriately expressed within the boundaries of marriage. We find many expressions of this love in the Old Testament[25] and the New Testament.[26]

Agape. Perhaps the most recognizable word for love that Christians are familiar with is that of *agape.* The Greek word for "love" in Galatians 5:22 is *agape.* Unlike the other words, this word is a purely biblical word. In its uses within scripture, we find it used in correlation with God and Jesus. In 1 John 4:7-8 (NIV), the love that comes from God is the same word we find here in Galatians 5:22—*agape.* According to Strong's Exhaustive Concordance, *agape* love is the love we experience from God our Father.

Society has a problem with the idea of love. We all want to experience love at some level. We all want to be loved. We all want someone to love. We are in love with the idea of love. We make movies about love, and we write songs about love. We throw

23   Romans 12:10; 1 Thessalonians 4:9; Hebrews 13:1; 1 Peter 1:22; 2 Peter 1:7 King James Version.

24   1 Samuel 18:1

25   Song of Solomon 1:2-4

26   Hebrews 13:4

the word "love" around a lot. We say things like, "I love that song," or "I love that restaurant," or "I love coffee." We even go so far to love objects and say, "I love my car." Sometimes, we "love" people based on a facade represented in the media despite having never met them.

There are many things that complicate what love truly is. Originally, God intended for us to have a pure meaning of the word "love". Love should be derived from the *agape* love we described above.

Here is the core of the matter: whatever way we were taught to love is the way we most likely will love others. The reason we don't fully understand love is that our idea of love is based on our experiences of love. If our experiences of love stemmed from healthy models of love, then we can model that same love forward.

Some of us never experienced healthy love. We didn't have a mom or dad that loved us like a child deserves to be loved. We never experienced the secure love of a parent. And since we never experienced a secure love of a parent, we struggle to offer a healthy (storge) love to others. This cycle continues from generation to generation.

Our experiences can produce unhealthy and distorted expressions of love. As children, some individuals may have grown up seeing their mother and father in a toxic or abusive relationship. In turn, their romantic relationship becomes toxic or abusive, and they view it as normal because it was their only model of romantic (eros) love.

Yet others might have been bullied or mistreated by multiple friends in their past and, therefore, find it difficult to trust others.

These experiences have taught them to keep others at arm's length. As a result, they are unable to confide in any individuals. This distrust can extend from friendships to co-workers, and even to church communities, never allowing the individual to settle in one place. Their lack of experience of brotherly love (philia) has wounded them.

The key is to realign, if you will, our concept of love. The afore-mentioned loves—storge, philia, and eros—are conditional. They are offered and given to us by people. People aren't perfect, so these types of love cannot offer perfection. When we place our trust in others' ability to give love, we are bound to experience disappointment.

> There is a real love. This real love is unconditional. It is not subject to anything that we could say or do. And, when we experience this love, it aligns all the other loves.

When we experience this real love, it will influence all other loves. This is why Paul puts LOVE first in Galatians 5:22. Because God's love is REAL love. It is not the sensationalized love in the movies, or the abusive love you experienced in your past, or even the conditional love in your current relationship. No, this is real love.

The biblical concept of agape love is God loving us. "*This is real love—not that we loved God, but that he loved us and sent his Son as a sacrifice to take away our sins,*" (1 John 4:10 NLT). We didn't have to do anything to earn this love. Real love is love given freely without expecting anything in return.

Agape love is God loving us despite our condition. *"But God showed his great love for us by sending Christ to die for us while we were still sinners,"* (Romans 5:8 NLT). Even when we were still in sin, God continued to love us. And he demonstrated that love by sending Jesus. Imagine trying to love someone who spits in your face or calls you names or turns their back on you. Would you continue to love them anyway? God did, and He still does. This is real love.

There is a saying that says, "Hurt people hurt people." Often-times, this is a true statement. Broken love will produce broken love. Song of Solomon 8:4 (NLT) says, *"Promise me, O women of Jerusalem, not to awaken love until the time is right."* There is a right time to awaken love in our lives. If we don't first experience God's unconditional love, we don't have a good foundation of love. Therefore, we can't give forward healthy love. It is vital to experience God's love because it will straighten our perspective on love.

There is a second part to that saying, "Hurt people hurt people," and it is "Loved people love people." 1 John 3:1a (NIV) says, *"See what great love the Father has lavished on us, that we should be called children of God!"* I love this version because it says "lavished". God not only loves you, but He lavishes you with love. It is a generous and extravagant love that never runs out. When I think of the word "lavish", I think of hand cream. Have you ever squeezed too much cream out of the tube, and since it's too hard to put back in, you offer it to someone else? That's how God's love is. You have so much of it that you offer the extra to others. You become so well loved by the Father that you begin to share that love over others, and you soon begin to see the changes in your relationships.

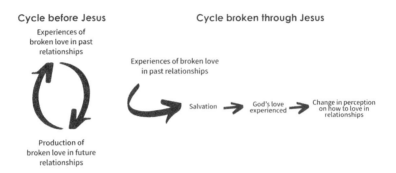

Illustration 3. God's Love Breaks the Cycle

Earlier we talked about how absorbing good things produces good fruit (see Illustration 2). Illustration 3 provides a more detailed graphic on how brokenness in us produces brokenness, but when we come to know Jesus, God begins to cover our past with His love. *"Most important of all, continue to show deep love for each other, for love covers a multitude of sins,"* (1 Peter 4:8 NLT). The love of God interrupts and breaks the ugly cycle of brokenness, and because of it, we begin to find healing.

The Bible has quite a few examples of how early experiences in life can cause broken love and unhealthy repeated cycles from generation to generation. In John 4:7-30, we read about the woman at the well. The story begins with Jesus leaving Judea, which was south. His destination was a three-day journey to Galilee. As Jesus and the disciples traveled, they became weary and stopped at the halfway point near Samaria. The Jews did not get along with the Samaritans, so they would go to many lengths to avoid going through Samaria; they would go around it through the Jordan River, extending their journey just to avoid coming into contact with a Samaritan. It would have been expected for Jesus and His disciples to pick the route alongside the Jordan River, but Jesus always does things differently. He decided to stop in a city in Samaria called Sychar and waited there while the disciples went out for food. Sychar was a place known for its wells—Jacob's well, to be precise. Jesus was about to use what was a normal, daily occurrence to reach a woman stuck in a cycle of brokenness.

The Bible says that it was about the sixth hour.[27] Other Bible versions place the time at noon.[28] This meant it was most likely the hottest time of day. It was not the norm for the women to go to the well at the hottest time of day; they would typically rise early and go to the well during the cool of the morning. After all, getting water from a well and dragging the day's portion back to their homes was an involved job. But this woman was no ordinary woman. She was an outcast of society. Her past and present was not something the rest of the townspeople would have wanted to be associated with. Yet, Jesus had a purpose. He chose to extend His love to her. It's interesting to note that Jesus was alone here. This is something that a Jewish man would never do, even more so with a Samaritan woman.

"Will you give me a drink?"[29] He carefully pieced together words that would lead to the right conversation. That conversation would eventually reveal that this woman was one whose past experiences led to a pattern of unhealthy relationships. Jesus, with gentleness and love, revealed that this woman "*had five husbands, and the man you now have is not your husband,*" (John 4:18 NIV). How many of us need an encounter like this with Jesus? When we encounter Him, there is so much love, but there is also truth.

27   John 4:6 King James Version.
28   John 4:6 New International Version.
29   John 4:7 New International Version.

A few verses later, Jesus reveals that He is the Messiah.[30] This truth changes everything for the Samaritan woman. You see, by revealing that He is the Messiah, He offered this woman hope. Surely, they were familiar with Old Testament prophecies and promises of the Messiah. The man who has come to save the world actually sat at the well, spoke with her, and offered her water so she would never thirst again (John 4:13-14 NLT). Here's how we know that the cycle in this woman's life was broken that day: *"Many Samaritans from the village believed in Jesus because the woman had said, "He told me everything I ever did,"* (John 4:39 NLT).

God's love will change everything. Jesus showed her real love that was nothing like what other men wanted from her. This love was different. It was the agape love of the Father. It was unconditional love. He offered her the kind of love that isn't toxic. It was pure. It was real. It was forever, and it didn't expect anything in return.

In summary, when we experience real love inwardly, we can give love outwardly. When we experience God's unconditional love, we can offer the same to others. This is a recipe for a healthy love relationship.

Inward Fruit: Joy

The next fruit listed is joy. This fruit is listed right after love because, when we experience love, it leads to joy. Indeed, all the fruit of the Spirit are intertwined, each carefully making room for another because it is the same Holy Spirit working and growing multiple fruit in us, often at the same time.

---

30   John 4:26

The Greek word for "joy" that Paul uses in Galatians 5:22 is *chara,* and it is defined as "calm delight". Strong's Exhaustive Concordance further notes that joy would have been understood by the readers of the book of Galatians as to be *exceeding.* This can help us understand three major points about joy.

Joy is not happiness. Whereas joy contributes to happiness, it is not the same thing. Happiness is a human emotion; joy comes from the Spirit. Happiness is natural; joy is supernatural. The confusion between the two stems from the fact that the English language fuses the two words to mean one. Merriam-Webster's Online Dictionary defines joy as "a feeling of great happiness"[31] and further defines happiness as "the state of well-being and contentment; joy".[32]

Although some Bible versions use the word "happy", if we look at the original Greek lexicon of the New Testament, we will find that the word "happy" or *makarios* is best translated as "blessed" as per Strong's Exhaustive Concordance. For this reason, we can conclude that the biblical definition of joy is not the same as the secular definition of joy. This is crucial when understanding the fruit of joy, and it leads to our next point.

Joy is not circumstantial. Earlier, we defined happiness as a "state of well-being and contentment", according to Merriam-Webster's dictionary. We can clearly see how happiness is dependent upon a "state of well-being". When we speak of the well-being of an individual, we are talking about a person's physical, emotional, and mental state. In other words, the three areas are factors that affect the condition of "happiness" in an individual. We know

---

31   Merriam-Webster.com Dictionary, s.v. "joy," accessed January 1, 2022, https://www.merriam-webster.com/dictionary/joy.

32   Merriam-Webster.com Dictionary, s.v. "happiness," accessed January 1, 2022, https://www.merriam-webster.com/dictionary/happiness.

that circumstances can vastly affect our state of well-being. If this is true, then happiness is affected by circumstances. If happiness is affected by circumstances, then happiness is not joy.

Happiness occurs when things go our way. If we win a game, get the job we wanted, or enjoy time with friends, feelings of happiness flow. When hard times come or pain is experienced, happiness ceases. This is because happiness is not only circumstantial, but it is also temporary. It is not meant to last a lifetime.

Joy occurs in every season of life. If we lose a game, are denied the job we wanted, or didn't get a chance to catch up with our friends, joy still exists. When hard times come or pain is experienced, joy continues. This is because joy is not circumstantial. It is unending.

The Word of God says that Jesus counted it as "joy" to endure the cross.[33] How can it be joy to endure pain? These seem like contradictory terms. In another scripture, James says to "count it all joy when you fall into various trials."[34] So when things become hard and trials occur, am I supposed to see this as an opportunity for joy? Yes. This is because joy is not based on our current circumstances, but rather on the hope that is before us, a hope that outweighs what we are going through. It is much like the hard work, time, effort, and money that you put into a kitchen renovation. It is a struggle, and at times, your emotions of weariness or anxiety may arise, but it can't take away your joy because you see the bigger picture. You see your dream kitchen, and as you work, this vision is in your mind. As we walk this journey with Jesus, struggles will come, but we see the vision in

---

33   Hebrews 12:2 New International Version
34   James 1:2 New King James Version

our minds of what Jesus has done for us, how He transformed us, and the hope He continues to offer us.

Jesus is the reason for our joy. We walk this journey because of Jesus. As we think of the salvation that we received because of Jesus' ultimate sacrifice on the cross, it should be a cause of great joy.

> *But the angel said to them, "Do not be afraid. I bring you good news that will cause great joy for all the people. Today in the town of David a Savior has been born to you; he is the Messiah, the Lord (Luke 2:10-11 NIV).*

Luke explains that the good news of the savior being born would be a cause for great joy. Luke is giving us a powerful tool. When we go through trials and tribulations, just think of Jesus and what He did for you. When circumstances try to steal your joy, remind yourself that Jesus is your joy.

It is so essential to allow the Spirit to work His fruit of joy over our life. There are many benefits to having this fruit planted and grown in your life. Nehemiah 8:10b (NIV) says, *"Do not grieve, for the joy of the Lord is your strength."* When we are grieving, God's joy will give us strength. In Psalm 30:5b (KJV), it says, *"...weeping may endure for a night, but joy cometh in the morning."* Although we may experience weeping, joy does not leave us. Lastly, in Psalm 16:11 (NIV) it says, *"You make known to me the path of life; you will fill me with joy in your presence, with eternal pleasures at your right hand."* As we walk this journey in the presence of God, He will fill us with His joy.

> When we begin to experience the joy of the Lord, we will do away with the unhealthy fruit of discontent.

Many of us have grown up with the belief that when we receive a gift or our physical wants are met, we will finally be happy. It is a deception to believe that objects and people can fill us. When we cannot achieve the satisfaction that we desire through people and things, we are filled with a deep discontent that drives us to do unstable things. And, when those unstable things, things like drugs, alcohol, sex, etc., cannot satisfy us, we fall into depression. This is why we need to understand the difference between joy and happiness. And we need to know that nothing in this world will ever satisfy us. Only the Father can give us the *inward* fruit of joy. Joy doesn't come from the outside; it comes from the inside.

Inward Fruit: Peace

The last of the "inward" fruit is peace. I used to think peace was a feeling that included a calmness around me, but after many life experiences, I now know that just as joy is not circumstantial, neither is peace.

The Greek word for "peace" that Paul uses in Galatians 5:22 is *eirene,* and it is defined as "the tranquil state of a soul assured of its salvation through Christ".[35] This gives us incredible insight to what Paul means when he lists this as a fruit of the Spirit. There

---

35   "G1515 – eirēnē – Strong's Greek Lexicon (kjv)." Blue Letter Bible. Accessed 3 Jan, 2022. https://www.blueletterbible.org/lexicon/g1515/kjv/tr/0-1/

is always a connection of the fruit of the Spirit to that of Jesus. Let's look at three things that will help us understand true peace.

Peace is the condition of your inside despite what is going on outside. We often think that a calm house, a tranquil job, or quietness is peace. Peace is not a calmness around me. It is a calmness within me, despite what is happening around me. A tree's fruit is not produced by its circumstances, and neither is peace produced by our circumstances. If we are rooted deeply in the Lord, we can withstand the storms that try to take away our peace.

Jesus said in John 16:33 (NIV), "*I have told you these things, so that in me you may have peace. In this world you will have trouble. But take heart! I have overcome the world.*" What? Peace and trouble? The King James Version uses the word "tribulation" instead of trouble.[36] Jesus understood that peace and circumstances are not mutually exclusive. This is why He made a point to let us know as well.

"In me you may have peace." This is a powerful phrase. We will not find peace in anyone other than Jesus. He is our peace. When we come to Him, the Holy Spirit will plant the seed of peace in us. Soon enough, we will see how different our response is amid tribulation, as we have the guidance of the Holy Spirit because we are now in Jesus. Our response will be tranquility even when our emotions want to take us elsewhere. Remember, the fruit of the Spirit helps us manage our emotions.

The peace of God is beyond our understanding. It is difficult to understand how we could remain calm and tranquil when things are unsettled. This is particularly difficult because our emotions can be strong, and our thoughts can consume us, as

---

36   John 16:33 King James Version.

we learned earlier. Revisiting the book *Anatomy of the Soul*, Dr. Curt Thompson states that, "The brain is constantly monitoring the landscape, both internally and externally, even when you are sleeping". He continues with great perception about our emotions:

> This constant monitoring and shifting in energy is the activity around which the brain organizes itself. This is emotion. The origin of our word emotion is grounded in the idea of e-motion, or preparing for motion. That is why the phenomenon of emotion is deeply tied to ongoing action or movement. We cannot separate what we feel from what we do.

This perception that Thompson offers is backed by research. We do have a hard time separating what we feel from what we do, and we don't need research to prove that to us. We have all experienced this. It is true. We have a hard time separating our feelings from our actions. This is precisely why we need the Holy Spirit. He can help us separate our feelings from our actions. So when a tribulation comes, He reminds us of the seed of peace He has planted in us.

Philippians 4:7 (NIV) says, *"And the peace of God, which transcends all understanding, will guard your hearts and your minds in Christ Jesus."* There is a peace that transcends all understanding. We cannot comprehend with our human brains how this peace takes over our heart and mind. It is only when we come to Jesus that the Holy Spirit interjects our anxieties and fears with His peace.

> ## Peace keeps my heart and mind from wandering.

It keeps my thoughts from running in stressful circles. Peace keeps me from feeling troubled, unsettled, and agitated. Peace keeps me from experiencing an unhealthy fear. It keeps me from being out of control, which stems from a lack of trust that God is in control.

Keep your mind on Him. Isaiah 26:3 (NLT) says, "*You will keep in perfect peace all who trust in you, all whose thoughts are fixed on you!*" It is a reminder of what we talked about earlier in chapter 2, taking hold of our negative thoughts by taking them captive to Jesus. And here in Isaiah, we find another tool to help us against thoughts that take away our peace—keeping our thoughts fixed on the Lord.

As a recap, these three inward fruits help us to be transformed inwardly, in our hearts and minds. The fruit of the Holy Spirit will undo all the past pain and rejection that harmed us inside, so that we can learn to produce fruit on the outside. We need the Holy Spirit because He is the restorer of all things.

CHAPTER SIX

THE FRUIT OF THE SPIRIT: OUTWARD FRUIT

But the Holy Spirit produces this kind of fruit in our lives: love, joy, peace, patience, kindness, goodness, faithfulness,gentleness, and self-control. There is no law against these things!

Galatians 5:22-23 NLT

As we discussed earlier, the fruit of the Spirit can be split into three sections. Each section helps us in different ways. We learned that the inward fruit are crucial because they help us to become transformed into a more mature believer as we experience them.

Moving forward, it is also important to experience the next group of fruit, the outward fruit. Not all the fruit we bear are meant to be eaten alone. A great sign of maturity is when we show that change outwardly. Outward fruit are fruit that we bear yet give to others. The three fruits in this category are patience, kindness, and goodness.

Outward Fruit: Patience

The fruit of patience is the first of what I call the outward fruit. These are called outward because we demonstrate them to others. You have heard the saying, "Oh, Lord, give me patience!" Patience is perhaps the most requested fruit in times of irritability.

The word "patience" in Galatians 5:22 is oftentimes translated as "longsuffering."[37] In its original Greek, longsuffering is *makrothymia*. According to Strong's Greek Lexicon, *makrothymia* comes from the root word *makrothymos*. This is important because the first part of this Greek word is *makro,* meaning "long", and the second part of the word *thymos* means "temper".[38] This breakdown of the word helps us to understand that, when we talk about patience, we are really talking about our temper. Let's dive in and look at three basic biblical concepts of the word *makrothymia* that give us a clear idea of what patience is.

Patience is the ability to control my temper when I am tested. We have all been there. We have had the experience of losing control of our temper. Someone does something, anger arises, and

---

37   Galatians 5:22 King James Version.

38   "G3116 – makrothymōs – Strong's Greek Lexicon (kjv)." Blue Letter Bible. Accessed 4 Jan, 2022. https://www.blueletterbible.org/lexicon/g3116/kjv/tr/0-1/

before you know it, you are reacting without thinking clearly. This is why it is essential to rely on the Holy Spirit. The Holy Spirit helps us control our temper.

One of the most notable Bible verses about anger is found in Ephesians 4:26 (NIV), *"In your anger do not sin: Do not let the sun go down while you are still angry."* Anger is not the culprit here. It is how we react when angry that is the matter. That is why this scripture says, *"in your anger do not sin,"* because God knew that we would experience anger as humans. Emotions are not bad. It is what we do with emotions that can be sinful.

Even Jesus was angry at times. In Mark 3:1-5, Jesus was in the synagogue and had encountered a man whose hand was shriveled up. There were others in the synagogue, too. And they were intently looking at Jesus to see if He would heal the man on the Sabbath. You see, it was not lawful to heal on the Sabbath. Jesus knew what they were thinking. He knew they were looking to accuse Him of wrongdoing. In verse 5, it says, *"He looked around at them in anger."*[39] Jesus was angry, and it even caused Him to be distressed. He did not react to that anger. He continued to focus on healing the man's shriveled hand.

Anger is not a weakness. It is a sign that something is bothering us, but we do not have to react in a way that is sinful. Cloud and Townsend in their book *Boundaries* state that "anger is a friend" and that "it was created by God for a purpose: to tell us that there's a problem that needs to be confronted." This is why we need to exercise the fruit of patience.

Patience is exercising an adequate time of waiting before expressing the anger you feel. Anger can lead to a bad temper.

---

39   Mark 3:5 New International Version

But when we allow the Holy Spirit to come into our lives and take control, He helps us slow down, think, and do the right thing. Ecclesiastes 7:9 (NIV) says, *"Do not be quickly provoked in your spirit, for anger resides in the lap of fools."* Stop, think, and give time for the Holy Spirit to help you to be patient.

Patience is the ability to bear things without losing control or giving up. In our first point about patience, we said that the Holy Spirit helps us to control our temper. In this point, we say the Holy Spirit helps us to continue. Patience is not only exercised in the moment but is necessary for the long haul. That is longsuffering. Patience is the ability to endure and persevere when hard times come. It helps me to stay planted and steady in the Father.

There is another word that the English language translates as patience, and it is found in Hebrews 10:36 (KJV), *"For ye have need of patience."* However, the Greek word for patience here is not *makrothymia*, but rather *hypomonē*, as noted in Strong's Exhaustive Concordance. Although this is not the Greek word found in Galatians, it still is valuable to discuss. *Makrothymia* relates to the patience we should have with others, and that is why it is an outward fruit of the Spirit. *Hypomonē* relates to the patience we should have in trials and sufferings. We need them both. The Holy Spirit plants the seed of patience in our lives. The former, *makrothymia*, is a patience that helps us grow in our character towards others when faced with testing and temptations (James 1:12). The latter, *hypomonē*, helps us grow in our faith toward God amid testing and temptations.

At times in our lives, we will be stretched through circumstances. But being stretched through circumstances is the only way to practice patience.[40] Stretching is the place in between where you

---

40   James 1:3 King James Version

were and where you are going and the thing that will sustain you is the fruit of patience given by the Holy Spirit.

Patience is the ability to wait when I'm anxious to do something. In our first point about patience, we said that the Holy Spirit helps us to control our temper. In the second point, we said the Holy Spirit helps us to continue. And in this final point, we say that the Holy Spirit keeps us from making the wrong moves.

The opposite of patience is impatience. When we become impatient, we do things we never thought we would do. A lot of people make unhealthy decisions because of a lack of patience. Impatience is triggered when we have a goal and realize that there are obstacles that are impeding our ability to achieve that goal. In efforts to get our goal back on track, we make moves outside of the will of God. Patience helps us to slow down and wait on the Lord.

> Impatience also produces a kind of fruit of its own. It motivates us to reduce our standards because impatience screams, "I want it now!"

So we lower our standards in relationships, careers, and our callings. Sarah and Abraham were impatient.[41] God promised them a child in their old age, and when that promise took too long for them, they decided to help God out. That impatience produced a fruit that complicated family dynamics forever.

---

41   Genesis 15-16.

We find another example of impatience in Esau. Esau sold his birthright because he was hungry.[42] Momentary stress and circumstances tend to create an anxiousness that leads us to make swift decisions without thinking things through. This impatience produced permanent consequences in the life of Esau.

When we are patient, we are showing the world that God is in control of our lives and that the Holy Spirit is in us. It is the Holy Spirit that produces a patience in us that empowers us to control our temper when we are tested, to overcome our desire to lose control, and to wait patiently before the Lord.

Outward Fruit: Kindness and Goodness

Often referred to as "the twin fruit" or "cousins", kindness and goodness are coupled together because one is reflective of the other. While they can operate on their own, they can also function together. Let's look at them separately and see how they work together.

Kindness

Kindness in the scriptures is also referred to as "gentleness".[43] In its original Greek, kindness is *chrēstotēs*. According to Strong's Greek Lexicon, *chrēstotēs* means "usefulness, i.e. morally, excellence (in character or demeanor): gentleness, good(-ness), kindness".[44] That is a lot to take in. Kindness carries with it many things, but most notably, it carries with it the idea of character

---

42   Genesis 25:29-34.
43   Galatians 5:22 King James Version.
44   "G5544 – chrēstotēs – Strong's Greek Lexicon (kjv)." Blue Letter Bible. Accessed 5 Jan, 2022. https://www.blueletterbible.org/lexicon/g5544/kjv/tr/0-1/

and demeanor. There is an innate sense of moral character when we practice the fruit of kindness.

Kindness is more than just being nice. I don't have to like someone to be nice to them. As a matter of fact, we are often nice to people who we don't like. Other times, we do something nice to someone without any regard to who they are and what their deeper needs are. Nice is when you are polite to people or treat people well. Being nice is not a bad thing; it's just not necessarily God-driven. Expressing kindness is when you care about people, and you show you care. Kindness is a fruit of the Spirit. It is Spirit-developed, Spirit-driven, and Spirit-directed. Let's observe some key points about kindness.

Kindness is Spirit-developed, Spirit-driven, and Spirit-directed. It is an awareness triggered by the Holy Spirit that helps us see a moment of need and step in with compassion. How many biblical examples of this do we see exemplified by Jesus? Jesus healed the sick, the outcasts, the sinners, and the rejected. He saw moments of need and always stepped in with compassion.

Jesus healed the sick, the outcasts, the sinners, and the rejected. Mark 5:25-32 tells the story of a woman who suffered from an issue of blood for twelve years. She had spent all the money she had to find healing, but her condition just got worse. When she heard that Jesus was passing through town, she ran after him to touch his garment. She had enough faith to know that if she could just touch even the hem of his garment, she would be "made whole". It was a little complicated, though. There was a bit of a crowd, but she reached out and touched Jesus and was immediately healed.[45] But it is what Jesus does after the woman is healed that embodies kindness. He sensed that someone had

---

45   Mark 5:25-34.

touched Him. Let's be straightforward here—during biblical times, Jewish men would not have touched a woman who was not his wife, and it was a disgrace for a woman to touch a man who was not her husband, especially if that woman had an issue of blood. Jesus didn't scold her. He didn't give her a long, drawn-out lecture. He just extended kindness with His word saying, "*Daughter, your faith has made you well. Go in peace. Your suffering is over,*" (Mark 5:34 NLT).

Kindness is the active, outward expression of love. Remember how we said that it was no coincidence that Paul listed the fruit of love first? This is because, though love is an inward fruit that we experience in God, it expresses itself outwardly as love, but also as kindness. When we demonstrate kindness, we are also demonstrating love. Jesus expressed kindness because the love of the Father and the empowerment of the Holy Spirit were working in Him. When we come to Jesus, he leads us to the love of the Father and the Holy Spirit makes a home in us. This is how we begin developing the fruit. As Christians, when we exercise kindness, even when some people don't deserve it, we are demonstrating to others that there is a God who loves them.

Goodness

Many people confuse kindness and goodness. They are related. Goodness in its original Greek is *agathōsynē*. According to Strong's Greek Lexicon, *agathōsynē* means "uprightness of heart".[46] Kindness carries with it the idea of moral character, and goodness carries with the idea of integrity. Let's look at some key similarities and differences between kindness and goodness.

---

46   "G19 – agathōsynē – Strong's Greek Lexicon (kjv)." Blue Letter Bible. Accessed 5 Jan, 2022. https://www.blueletterbible.org/lexicon/g19/kjv/tr/0-1/

Kindness vs. goodness and the quality of doing right. One of the key similarities of both kindness and goodness is that they both emphasize doing what is right. The difference is in that kindness is the quality of doing right by others; goodness is the quality of doing right by God.

We practice kindness when we do what is right to others despite our differences. Let's say that you were wronged by someone. They spread a false narrative of you. Time passes, and you see the person. They are pulled over to the side of the road, their family in the back seat. Their car is not working, and it is very cold and rainy outside. Do you pass them by, or do you offer to help? What is right in this case? Many people might say to pass them by. Truly, what would Jesus do? Jesus would be kind. I can guarantee that. Kindness would not pass them by. Kindness would pull over and bless them.

God expects that we extend the same kindness He extended to us. Romans 11:22 (NIV) says, *"Consider therefore the kindness and sternness of God: sternness to those who fell, but kindness to you, provided that you continue in his kindness. Otherwise, you also will be cut off."* Consider the kindness of God if we continue in that kindness.

We practice goodness when we do what is right by God's standards despite the world's differences. Practicing goodness is living with integrity. It means we have strong moral principles. When the world asks you to do something that goes against God's standards, and you choose what is right by God, that is the fruit of goodness working in you. Let's say your best friend is late for work and asks you to lie to the boss for them. You may find yourself at a crossroad between doing what is right by your friend and doing what is right by God. Always choose God. Goodness would react by telling your friend that you cannot lie for them because you are a Christian. Goodness would decide based on God's standards.

Kindness and goodness both demonstrate that we care. When we practice kindness, we demonstrate to people that we care about them. It tells them that we took the time to *see* them and their needs. It shows the world that God is at work in us. When we practice goodness, it demonstrates to God that we care about Him. It tells God that we are paying attention to Him. This shows God that His work in us is not in vain.

Returning solely to goodness...

Goodness is an awareness triggered by the Holy Spirit that helps us see a moment and step in with God's truth. We react to all moments with God's word and respond with God's truth.

Jesus healed the sick, the outcasts, the sinners, and the rejected, and that was the kind thing to do, but He also stepped in with truth. John 8:1-11 tells the story of a woman who was about to be stoned because she had been caught in adultery. Jesus didn't scold her. He didn't lecture her. He intervened, and the accusers who were about to stone her walked away. That was kindness working in Jesus. However, we also see one crucial phrase in this passage where Jesus exemplifies goodness by telling the adulterous woman, "Go now and leave your life of sin."[47] Jesus also speaks truth.

Recapping, Jesus is the greatest example of both kindness and goodness working together. We need to have both working in our lives. And they both work best together.

---

47   John 8:11 New International Version.

Kindness without goodness is like a bandage
that stops the wound from bleeding (the current
circumstance), but it does not treat the infection (the
sin). Goodness without kindness is like a stinging
antiseptic that treats the infection (the sin) but doesn't
help protect the wound from pain (the current
circumstance). Kindness and goodness when working
together help stop the bleeding (the circumstance)
and infection (the sin).

This is what Jesus did; Jesus stopped our pain with His kindness, and He healed our infections with His goodness. And now we take those seeds of kindness and goodness that were planted in our lives and share the fruit of the Spirit forward with others by extending kindness and goodness.

THE FRUIT OF THE SPIRIT: ONWARD FRUIT

But the Holy Spirit produces this kind of fruit in
our lives: love, joy, peace, patience, kindness,
goodness, faithfulness, gentleness, and self-control.
There is no law against these things!

Galatians 5:22-23 NLT

We experience the fruit of the Spirit that changes us. We show others that change in us by practicing the fruit that is working in us. But we don't just consume and give to others to consume. We also take the seeds that are in our fruit and plant them to make more fruit. That's part of the maturity process, recognizing that what we have comes from our Creator.

The way we give back to God is by taking the seed found in the fruit we bear and planting it to produce more for the kingdom. Onward fruit is the fruit that keeps us moving forward in the Lord. The three fruits in this category are faithfulness, gentleness, and self-control.

Onward Fruit: Faithfulness

Faithfulness is challenging because it has a two-fold meaning. Some biblical versions label it as "faith"[48], and others label it as "faithfulness"[49] in context. In its original Greek, faithfulness is *pistis*. According to Strong's Greek Lexicon, *pistis* can mean both "faith" and "one who is full of faith"[50], as in faithfulness. Thayer's Greek Lexicon gives two clear definitions that will help us understand the two-fold meaning of the fruit of faithfulness.[51] Thayer lists the first definition of *pistis* as a "a conviction or belief respecting man's relationship to God and divine things", whereas the second definition is listed as "fidelity, faithfulness, i.e. the character of one who can be relied on". One speaks of a conviction and the other speaks of a character.

Conviction vs character. The fruit of faithfulness first plants in us a deep conviction in God while also shaping our character and making us faithful to God. We know that God is real, so we live for Him. Conviction is something we have; character is what we display.

---

48   Galatians 5:22 King James Version.
49   Galatians 5:22 New International Version.
50   "G4102 – pistis – Strong's Greek Lexicon (kjv)." Blue Letter Bible. Accessed 6 Jan, 2022. https://www.blueletterbible.org/lexicon/g4102/kjv/tr/0-1/
51   "Abbreviations in Thayer's Lexicon, Etc. – Study Resources." Blue Letter Bible. Accessed 6 Jan, 2022. https://www.blueletterbible.org/study/misc/thayers.cfm

Faith. Faith is biblically defined in Hebrews 11:1 (NLT) as, *"Faith shows the reality of what we hope for; it is the evidence of things we cannot see."* This is the best definition of faith that exists because it was penned by the Creator. We can learn a lot from this verse.

First, faith begins with hope.

> *Against all hope, Abraham in hope believed and so became the father of many nations, just as it had been said to him, "So shall your offspring be." Without weakening in his faith, he faced the fact that his body was as good as dead—since he was about a hundred years old—and that Sarah's womb was also dead. Yet he did not waver through unbelief regarding the promise of God, but was strengthened in his faith and gave glory to God, being fully persuaded that God had power to do what he had promised (Romans 4:18-21 NIV).*

Abraham, despite a moment of impatience, is described as the father of faith in the scriptures. He exercised hope, which led to faith. I really love how verse 18 says *"against all hope, Abraham in hope believed"*. This verse is saying that, when things looked hopeless to Abraham, he hoped anyway. He believed anyway. Abraham was older, and so was his wife. They had no children when he received a promise from God that he would be the father of many nations. Without weakening in his faith, he continued to believe, which was an exercise of his faith, and he became the father of many nations.

Second, faith continues with an unwavering belief. Faith isn't something that takes away all your troubles; it helps you get through them. Faith helps us through hard moments of our life. It keeps us from wavering in our beliefs. There is a certainty that accompanies faith. This is the conviction part. Even when the enemy tries to plant seeds of unbelief and doubt, we hold tight to our conviction that God is God, and nothing can stop His promises over us. 2 Corinthians 1:20 (NLT) says, *"For all of God's promises have been fulfilled in Christ with a resounding 'Yes!' And through Christ, our 'Amen' (which means "Yes") ascends to God for his glory."*

Third, hope leads to faith, and faith leads to faithfulness. We can't exercise faith unless we come to know Jesus, who is the author and the finisher of our faith.[52] When we come to accept Jesus, the Holy Spirit comes into our lives and plants seeds of faith that deepen our conviction with faith and strengthens our character with faithfulness.

Faithfulness. Earlier, we defined faithfulness as the character of one who can be relied upon. We have discussed how the fruit of the Spirit are not emotions, but rather, they are characteristics, attributes, and qualities that help us manage our emotions. We must allow the Holy Spirit to plant the seed of faith in us, so that we become a person of character. When we speak of the character of someone in this context, we are speaking of what this person is known for—a person who will continue to believe even when the outside circumstances are saying otherwise. Faithfulness is the application or product of our faith. If we say we have faith, then it should be evident in how we live.

Now, in a perfect world, we would all have unwavering faith. In a perfect world, we would all exemplify faithfulness. However, this is just not how it is. Life's circumstances can bruise our trust. Maybe you grew up with a father who left you. Maybe your mother promised lots of things and never followed through. Maybe you were in a relationship where your significant other

---

52   Hebrews 12:2 King James Version.

cheated on you. In the end, because of those experiences, we can find it difficult to trust, believe, and have faith in people. And that lack of trust can be redirected toward God.

The opposite of faith is unbelief. The root of unbelief is doubt based on our past experiences. Even Jesus said in Matthew 21:21 (NIV), *"Jesus replied, "Truly I tell you, if you have faith and do not doubt, not only can you do what was done to the fig tree, but also you can say to this mountain, 'Go, throw yourself into the sea,' and it will be done."* Doubt can interfere with our faith. Doubt is the product of destructive, unchallenged, and unchanged thoughts (Hawkins and Clinton 2015, 89). When we experience something in the present that reminds us of something in the past, it can trigger how that circumstance made us feel and cause us to react to the present as if it was the past. A floodgate of memories and emotions surface, and our instinct is to protect ourselves emotionally and mentally, so that we do not duplicate the suffering. We need to be aware of how our past might affect our faith in God.

Faith in Jesus can change this situation. Hawkins and Clinton, authors of *The New Christian Counselor* say, "When a person expresses faith in Christ, the Holy Spirit comes as a divine light to conquer death and dispel darkness." The Holy Spirit helps us to be faithful. He helps us to keep the commitment of faith we made through Jesus Christ.[53] This means we are faithful in our commitment, which carries over into our lifestyle in the following ways:

1. *We remain steadfast.* A byproduct of faith is being steadfast in the Lord. We remain steadfast in Him. Nothing

---

53   Romans 5:1-2 New King James Version

moves us because we have a strong faith in God. When we are steadfast, we are showing that we are faithful to God.

Therefore, my dear brothers and sisters, stand firm. Let nothing move you. Always give yourselves fully to the work of the Lord, because you know that your labor in the Lord is not in vain (1 Corinthians 15:58 NIV).

2. *We have deeds reflective of faith.* Another byproduct of faith is deeds. James says that faith without deeds (things that we do outwardly) is dead. It's important to note that we are saved by grace through faith in Jesus. Deeds do not save us, but they reflect our faith. This passage shows us that faith brings about deeds, not the other way around. But rather than give you examples, let's go to the Scriptures.

What good is it, my brothers and sisters, if someone claims to have faith but has no deeds? Can such faith save them? Suppose a brother or a sister is without clothes and daily food. If one of you says to them, "Go in peace; keep warm and well fed," but does nothing about their physical needs, what good is it? In the same way, faith by itself, if it is not accompanied by action, is dead. But someone will say, "You have faith; I have deeds." Show me your faith without deeds, and I will show you my faith by my deeds. You believe that there is one God. Good! Even the demons believe that—and shudder. You foolish person, do you want evidence that faith without deeds is useless? Was not our father Abraham considered righteous for what he did when he offered his son Isaac on the altar? You see that his faith and his actions were working together, and his faith was made complete by what he did. And the scripture was fulfilled that says, "Abraham believed God, and it was credited to him as righteousness,"and he was called

God's friend. You see that a person is considered righteous by what they do and not by faith alone. In the same way, was not even Rahab the prostitute considered righteous for what she did when she gave lodging to the spies and sent them off in a different direction? As the body without the spirit is dead, so faith without deeds is dead (James 2:14-26 NIV).

> ## Faithfulness will reward us.

There is a promise to those that remain faithful. This promise is not a byproduct; it is a reward for our faithfulness. The promise is the crown of life. The crown of life is the reward for our faithfulness in this life, especially in hard times, temptations, and pain. The Bible tells us to *"Be faithful, even to the point of death, and I will give you life as your victor's crown"* (Revelation 2:10 NIV).

Onward Fruit: Gentleness

When I was little, I loved to ride my bike. I have one strong memory of riding my bike when I was about six years old. I was only allowed to ride up and down the block, but I vividly remember going as fast as I could and almost making it to the end of the block when I hit a bump on the sidewalk. The bike went spinning in the air, and so did I. My knees hit the ground, and I instantly felt pain. I started bleeding and crying. Before I knew it, one of the teenage neighbors came over and gently picked me up and carried me over to my house, then he went back to get my bike. The most significant part of this memory was the gentleness my neighbor took in my moment of pain.

Gentleness, referred to as "meekness" in the King James Version, is the eighth fruit of the Spirit. In original Greek, it is *praotēs*. According to Strong's Greek Lexicon, *praotēs* means "mildness".[54] Some have interpreted gentleness as a weakness. Gentleness is meekness, not weakness. It is strength under control. It is the ability to be strong yet have a gentle touch. Just as in my example above, if you hurt your leg, you would want and need someone strong to pick you up. But they would also have to be gentle as to not cause more damage to your injury.

Jesus was a master at gentleness. He never boasted or flaunted physical strength. Paul describes Jesus as meek and gentle.[55] He most definitely displayed strength under control in so many instances, including death on the cross. Through it all, Jesus demonstrated the Spirit at work in Him as He treated those around Him with gentleness.

The Holy Spirit works in us this fruit of gentleness. Have you ever encountered someone who is abrasive? Some people can have a rough personality or demeanor, but when that person comes to Jesus, you see a powerful transformation in temperament. That's because, as we come to the Lord, the Holy Spirit is working in us, and we soon see things change.

54   "G19 – praotes – Strong's Greek Lexicon (kjv)." Blue Letter Bible. Accessed 5 Jan, 2022. https://www.blueletterbible.org/lexicon/g19/kjv/tr/0-1/
55   2 Corinthians 10:1 King James Version.

Deborah Denson, an expert in nonviolent communication, describes three characteristics of meekness or gentleness: yielded, teachable, and responsive.[56]

A person who is gentle is yielded. Jesus was often confronted by religious leaders, and in all instances, His strength was under control. When a person is yielded, they give way. Just as a yield sign causes you to give way to others, being guided by the Holy Spirit will prompt you to give way to arguments. Being gentle helps us avoid hostile attitudes and conflicts. Proverbs 19:11 (NIV) says, *"A person's wisdom yields patience; it is to one's glory to overlook an offense."* We can only yield with the help of the Holy Spirit.

A person who is gentle is teachable. Jesus was teachable. As a child, Jesus and His family had a custom to visit Jerusalem every year for Passover. When Jesus was twelve, His parents once again went down to visit. On the journey back home, His parents realized that He was not with them. They eventually found Him three days later and were astonished at what they found him doing. *"After three days they found him in the temple courts, sitting among the teachers, listening to them and asking them questions,"* (Luke 2:46 NIV). You read that right; Jesus was listening to them and asking them questions. Being teachable is significant to being gentle because teachability is the opposite of pride. Pride refuses to learn from others.

A person who is gentle is careful in their response. Jesus was always careful with His words. He wanted to be responsive to individuals and their needs. He also needed to be gentle to the naysayers around. This is what we need from the Holy Spirit.

56   "Meekness Is Really Power Under Control – Deborah Denson ...", n.d., accessed January 7, 2022, https://www.deborahdenson.com/meekness-really-power-control/.

We need His guidance to react and respond in gentle ways in all circumstances. The Holy Spirit helps us act out that gentleness to those in need and avoid being rude or discourteous to the naysayers around us. Proverbs 15:1 (NIV) says, *"A gentle answer turns away wrath, but a harsh word stirs up anger."*

> Jesus is the embodiment of gentleness. We are not only gentle to others because it is the right thing to do, but we are gentle to others because it shows them the character of Christ.

We represent Jesus to this world. There is a whole culture of people who claim to be Christians but are so abrasive that they turn people off from coming to Jesus. Let's be the Christians who win people to Jesus because our character under the power of the Holy Spirit draws them to Christ.

Onward Fruit: Self-Control

Paul wraps up the fruit of the Spirit with self-control. Self-control is also called temperance in the King James Version. In original Greek, it is *egkrateia*. According to Strong's Greek Lexicon, *egkrateia* means "the virtue of one who masters his desires and passions, especially his sensual appetites".[57] There is a sense of restraint that comes with the fruit of self-control. I believe "temperance" is a much better word because it implies passion

---

57   "G1466 – egkrateia – Strong's Greek Lexicon (kjv)." Blue Letter Bible. Accessed 8 Jan, 2022. https://www.blueletterbible.org/lexicon/g1466/kjv/tr/0-1/

controlled by the Spirit. "Self-control" implies that I am the one doing the controlling. The reality is that the Spirit of God helps us to resist the temptations that push us to be out of control.

Those who find themselves out of control have trouble with saying no to the things that can damage them, their marriages, their relationships, their finances, and most importantly, their walk with Jesus. We have been talking about Galatians 5:22-23 for a while, and now is the perfect time to look at these verses in greater context. When you get a chance, read all of Galatians 5.

Here is a quick breakdown of Galatians 5. Paul begins chapter 5 of Galatians with a reminder that we are free in Christ and a supplication to "*not let yourselves be burdened again by the yoke of slavery.*"[58] This yoke of slavery that Paul refers to is not about an actual slave serving someone; it is about how sin enslaves us. When we lack self-control, we fall to temptation. We have already studied the effects of temptation earlier. "*Temptation comes from our own desires, which entice us and drag us away. These desires give birth to sinful actions. And when sin is allowed to grow, it gives birth to death*" (James 1:14-15 NLT). If we continue this pattern, eventually, we become slaves to sin.

It is crucial to practice saying no to temptation. We can't think to ourselves, "Just this once." A few verses later in Galatians 5:9 (NIV), Paul writes, "*A little yeast works through the whole batch of dough.*" Throughout the Bible, we find yeast as a symbolism for sin. While in this context, Paul is referring to an issue of law—circumcised versus uncircumcised—this verse is still applicable to self-control. When we open the door even once to temptation, we run the risk of becoming controlled by the sin, rather than controlling the sin.

---

58   Galatians 5:1 New International Version.

Paul really breaks it down in Galatians 5:13 (NIV). He warns, *"Do not use your freedom to indulge the flesh."* We are free in Christ, but that freedom is not a license to keep on deliberately sinning. After all, if we keep on deliberately sinning, do we even know Jesus? First John 3:6 (NIV) answers this very question. *"No one who lives in him keeps on sinning. No one who continues to sin has either seen him or known him."*

If we know Jesus, then the Holy Spirit has come to live in us. Paul addressed this point in the book of 1 Corinthians 6:19-20 (NIV). *"Do you not know that your bodies are temples of the Holy Spirit, who is in you, whom you have received from God? You are not your own; you were bought at a price. Therefore honor God with your bodies."* The Holy Spirit is in us, which means that we do not have to battle temptation on our own.

Paul lays out the fundamental truth about what it means to live in the spirit in the verses that follow. How do you say no to temptation? By living in the Spirit.

> *So I say, walk by the Spirit, and you will not gratify the desires of the flesh. For the flesh desires what is contrary to the Spirit, and the Spirit what is contrary to the flesh. They are in conflict with each other, so that you are not to do whatever[c] you want. But if you are led by the Spirit, you are not under the law. The acts of the flesh are obvious: sexual immorality, impurity and debauchery; idolatry and witchcraft; hatred, discord, jealousy, fits of rage, selfish ambition, dissensions, factions and envy; drunkenness, orgies, and the like. I warn you, as I did before, that those who live like this will not inherit the kingdom of God. But the fruit of the Spirit is love, joy, peace, forbearance, kindness, goodness, faithfulness, gentleness and self-control. Against such*

things there is no law. Those who belong to Christ Jesus have crucified the flesh with its passions and desires. Since we live by the Spirit, let us keep in step with the Spirit (Galatians 5:16-25 NIV).

Walk by the Spirit, and you will not gratify the flesh. "Walk" here is defined as "to regulate one's life; to conduct oneself".[59] But it's not just walking, but rather, it is walking *by the Spirit*. We regulate ourselves with the helper, the Holy Spirit. We conduct ourselves according to the Spirit. Those that live an out-of-control lifestyle of sin will not "inherit the kingdom" of God (Galatians 5:21 NIV).

In modern society, we desperately need the fruit of self-control.

> Self-control is like a wall that protects a city.

Proverbs 25:28 (NIV) says, *"Like a city whose walls are broken through is a person who lacks self-control."* Walls in scripture represent protection. The spiritual application here is that, when we exercise self-control, we build spiritual walls around us (the city) and that protects us from falling prey to temptation.

We build those walls when we live a lifestyle of reading the Word, praying daily, and fasting regularly. When we feed our spirit with spiritual things, our spirit is not only stronger but more perceptive. The way you build muscles is by eating right,

59   "G4043 – peripateō – Strong's Greek Lexicon (kjv)." Blue Letter Bible. Accessed 8 Jan, 2022. https://www.blueletterbible.org/lexicon/g4043/kjv/tr/0-1/

working out, and getting plenty of rest; the way you build those spiritual muscles of self-control is by exercising your spirit.

Reading the word. Ephesians 6:17 (NIV) calls the Word of God the "sword of the Spirit". When we read the Word of God, it helps cut out the sin in our lives. It helps us clarify what is of the flesh and what is of the Spirit because *"the word of God is alive and active. Sharper than any double-edged sword, it penetrates even to dividing soul and spirit, joints and marrow; it judges the thoughts and attitudes of the heart"* (Hebrews 4:12 NIV). If you read the Word of God, it will awaken you to live in the Spirit. As it divides the flesh from the spirit, you begin to understand what is good, in turn strengthening your self-control.

Praying. Prayer is essential in the Christian walk because it is our communication to the Father. When you are feeling weak and ready to give in to the temptation, get on your knees and pray. Romans 8:26 (NIV) says, *"In the same way, the Spirit helps us in our weakness. We do not know what we ought to pray for, but the Spirit himself intercedes for us through wordless groans."* When we pray, the Spirit intercedes for us. He helps us in our weaknesses. Prayer makes us stronger in the spirit. Strength in the spirit produces self-control.

Fasting. There are some sinful habits that will require lots of prayer and fasting. Fasting is a tool that helps us focus. Jesus was led by the Spirit into the wilderness to be tempted by the devil in Matthew 4. You read that correctly. *The Spirit led Jesus into a wilderness to be tempted by the devil.* It was necessary for Jesus to experience temptation to leave us an example of how to overcome temptation. During this time, Jesus was "fasting for forty days and forty nights."[60] Fasting was the tool Jesus used to

---

60   Matthew 4:2 New International Version.

focus on God's will for His life and not give in to temptation. Fasting can also help you develop self-control. Fasting tells the flesh that the spirit is in control.

CHAPTER EIGHT

SEASONS AND REACHING MATURITY

⚔

There is a time for everything and a season
for every activity under the heaven.

Ecclesiastes 3:1 NIV

This journey to maturity is not always a straight line. There will be mountains, valleys, and rough terrain. There will be seasons where we will feel like giving up. There will be seasons that will shake, strip, and stretch us. We all go through seasons. Seasons are a necessary part of life that promote growth and maturity.

The word *season* is defined as a period that is distinguished by certain conditions to promote growth. Ecclesiastes demonstrates that seasons are appointed by God. Just as He created the seasons to promote growth in nature, He has appointed seasons in a man's life.

I have been through some difficult seasons in my life. Perhaps one day, I will share them in detail with the world. At times, the memory of tough seasons still causes a pain in my heart. But then I remember how God brought me out of that season. I can look back and see how much I have grown.

Every season is a possibility to grow. Unfortunately, we live in a broken world, and we will have to go through difficult times. Rather than looking at the season as a difficult one or a hard one, look at it and ask God what is it that He wants you to learn from this season that you will be able to carry forth towards the purpose and the plan He has for you in the future.

Revisiting the definition of *season* will give us more revelation and insight about whatever we are going through right now. Like we read earlier, *season* is defined as a period that is distinguished by certain conditions to promote growth.

A period. A time frame designated. A portion of time. Ecclesiastes 3:1 makes it clear that to everything there is a time. If you are living and breathing, you will go through times of change. The good news is that God is the keeper of time. And if He is the keeper of time, we can trust Him to work everything for our good (Rom. 8:28).

Certain conditions. Every season is distinguished by certain conditions. I really, really love summer. I am a teacher, so this is not only my time off, but it is also time to enjoy my family, to garden, and to bake, which are all things I love to do. But not all seasons are the same. Some seasons have fair weather and fun times; others have cold temperatures and dark days. One thing I know for sure is that, when the storms come, God is with me (Is. 41:10).

Promote growth. The more I observe nature, the more I come to realize the value of every season. Each season has a purpose. The result of each season is to produce a condition that leads to growth. You might not see the result at the moment, but God is always at work, and whatever you are going through is part of the process of growth and maturity.

There are a lot of Christians who are stuck in the same season. That's where stagnancy occurs and where we stay stuck in immaturity.

> Stuck people walk around with seeds in their pockets rather than in the ground. They do so because they don't want to die to self and live for Jesus.

What we put into every season and what we allow God to do in us during that season will define our result.

I live in Chicago, so we experience all four seasons at their height. After months of dark mornings and evenings with few sunny hours in between, spring is a welcomed arrival. What I love most about spring is that winter is over. And spring reminds me that something new is about to happen.

I spend a lot of those mild spring and summer days gardening. So, when spring arrives, it means it's time to plant. My husband and I just recently rebuilt our garden bed with the help of a friend. The old one had rotting wood and hard soil. So, we opted to rebuild one. We used solid materials and made sure to check with the professionals about what soil mix to use. We planted. We watered. We saw growth. In the end, we were able to harvest and enjoy the fruits of our labor.

One of the things I have learned is that, just as my garden goes through seasons of planting, growing, and harvesting, eventually there is a time that the garden is not producing due to the season. Up here in Chicago, you cannot grow during the cold winters. If you drive around, you will see trees that appear to be dead. They aren't dead. They have just shed their leaves in efforts to preserve as many nutrients and minerals as possible to make it through the freezing winter temperatures. As soon as the season changes, those same trees who once appeared dead begin to sprout and bud. Soon enough, those buds become leaves, and we begin to see fruit.

You will go through seasons that appear to be dead. But continue to absorb the minerals and nutrients you need to preserve your life. Continue to seek God in the difficult season. In due time, you will surely see something budding.

Now may He who supplies seed to the sower, and bread for food, supply and multiply the seed you have sown and increase the fruits of your righteousness

2 Corinthians 9:10 (NKJV)

Reaching Maturity

Everything we have been talking about has to do with maturity. We learned that maturity doesn't imply instant perfection. It implies that we are on a journey to that perfection. Jesus declares that we should be perfect. *"Be perfect, therefore, as your heavenly Father is perfect." (Matthew 5:48 NIV).*

The word here for perfect is, once again, *teleios*. Yes, we can reach perfection just as our heavenly Father is perfect. But we cannot do it on our own, and it is not immediate. In fact, we will not reach complete perfection until we are with Jesus in heaven, but we definitely can strive to be mature with the help of the Holy Spirit while here on earth.

We have learned that as believers, we are expected to grow. We have been given tools to help us grow out of infancy and into maturity. We discussed that we are a seed that needs to be planted and rooted deeply in Christ and that as we grow, the Holy Spirit is working His fruit in our lives for further transformational change. That transformational change will take us from who we were before Christ (lost and perhaps bitter or depressed) to how God has meant for us to live (in goodness, peace, and joy). This walk in Christ is a journey, and every step you take will get you closer to your destination of maturity. Don't give up. Don't give in. Don't look back.

> *God has given each of you a gift from his great variety of spiritual gifts. Use them well to serve one another. Do you have the gift of speaking? Then speak as though God himself were speaking through you. Do you have the gift of helping*

others? Do it with all the strength and energy that God sup-
plies. Then everything you do will bring glory to God through
Jesus Christ. All glory and power to him forever and ever!
Amen (1 Peter 4:10-11 NLT).

In Chapter 1, we started this book by citing 1 Corinthians 13:11 (NLT), "When I was a child, I spoke like a child and reasoned like a child. But when I grew up, I put away childish things." This means you must make some changes in your life. You will need to remind yourself to speak and think differently. You will need to resist the temptation to fall back into the old ways of thinking and acting.

Habits aren't formed overnight. We don't become conditioned by exercising once. We don't learn to play musical instruments in a day. So, we most certainly will not mature by just hoping to mature or practicing it for one week. The way we think affects our very maturity. That's why Paul says, you have to begin to think and reason differently. To make mature thinking a part of your life is going to require intentionality, consistency, and longevity. You must wake up every morning and decide to think and act differently. Then, you have to make it a lifetime habit.

Here is what a day could look like: Alarm rings.

Pray. This could be for five minutes or ten minutes. Then slowly increase your time if possible. In this prayer, ask the Holy Spirit to help you make the right choices. Ask Him to help keep your thoughts clean. Ask Him to help you stay focused on God. Ask for wisdom, knowledge, and understanding to deal with all issues that you may face. Prayer is effective. There are so many things that are avoided because our prayers block them. Prayer is also a conversation with the Father. Have you ever prayed for God to speak to you about something? Have you ever had to make a decision and in your desperation, you have called out to God to speak out, to speak loudly?

Over the years, I have learned that God always speaks to us in many different ways including His word and an audible voice. He hears us and He speaks to us. What I have also learned is this: If you are having a hard time hearing the voice of God, it is probably because there is too much noise around you. Psalm 5:3, "In the morning, O Lord, You will hear my voice; In the morning I will order my prayer to You and eagerly watch." Lower the volume around you for a moment and pray. Set your day up right and watch what the Lord will do.

After you pray, fill your mind with the Word of God. An empty mind is begging for fiery darts from the enemy or unwanted reminders of the past, but if you fill your mind with Scripture, you will experience a *living and active* word that will be activated throughout the whole day. When we read the Word of God, we are being proactive. We are training our minds for the moment of battle, so if anything pops up that tempts us to regress to our old ways, we are ready to fight with the Sword of the Spirit. As the day progresses, that word divides the soul (our emotions and thoughts) from the spirit (the part that connects with God) and we can easily discern how to deal with issues.

After you get ready, head out for work, or take the kids to school, it is a good idea to periodically do a check in the spirit in various ways. Read the Bible. Construct a consistent Bible reading habit. Constructing a habit generates a relationship between you and the word in a way that creates an influence in your mind and soul. This idea goes back to what we talked about earlier - taking the thoughts captive by stopping the thought and replacing it with Scripture. Memorize and internalize the word. Memorizing the word is a weapon; internalizing it makes it a sword. We can pull that verse out swiftly when the mind won't stop, or the enemy rises against us. You should also take time to talk to God. He is there to hear you vent. He is a listening ear. According to the Gospel Coalition, nearly half of the Psalms are laments before the Lord. That means that there are lots of Psalms in the Bible where the author is crying out to God and God is listening. And He is there to hear you, too. I also like to have a worship playlist ready to go. There is so much power in praise and worship. If you can, put your headphones on or turn your speakers up to worship the worry away and praise the enemy into confusion. Your praise will reset your mind and remind you of the goodness of God. Worship will allow you to release what is in your heart and focus on Jesus.

If you find yourself being challenged throughout the day, lean into the Holy Spirit. Ask Him to guide you. Remember that he is here to help us. He is available, with all His fruit, to help us control our emotions. Many make the mistake of thinking that difficult days disappear when you mature. They don't. What changes is your capacity to overcome. You learn to be proactive and store up reserves for tough times. You learn how to respond differently than before. You learn to tap into the tools you learned. And, above all, you learn that you have the support of the Holy Spirit. I always say He is my best friend. He is your best friend, too.

As you wind down your day of work outside or inside of your home, think about all the good things that God did for you. Thank Him for those moments. Reflect on the tough things you went through, learn from them but don't live there. If your church has a mid-week service, I highly recommend that you attend. If it's the weekend, make church a priority. When the Scripture says, 'Better is one day in Your courts than a thousand elsewhere,' it is absolutely true. Although God is everywhere, there is something about going into a place that is fully reserved for His presence. The Bible says in Psalm 16, "You make known to me the path of life; in your presence there is fullness of joy; at your right hand are pleasures forevermore." So, when you are down, His presence can lift you up. As an added value to going to the house of the Lord, we find strength in numbers. Jesus said in Matthew 18:19, "If two of you agree here on earth concerning anything you ask, my Father in heaven will do it for you." If you are feeling weak, ask your church to pray with you.

While the words of this book have come to an end, the Holy Spirit is with you forever. It is my hope for you that you would make room for the Holy Spirit to work in your mind, soul, and spirit so that you can become everything that God has called you to be, just as I did so many years ago. So, decide to surrender to the Holy Spirit and GROW UP ALREADY! As you do, the Holy Spirit will transform, deliver, and empower you into maturity.

BE BLESSED!

BIBLIOGRAPHY

Strong, James. (1990). *The New Strong's Exhaustive Concordance of the Bible*. Nashville, TN: T. Nelson Publishers. (pp. 188, 885, 1005, 997-998, 136, 388, 660, 571, 806, 805, 582, 429, 341, 395, 1040, 453, 384).

Vine, W. E., Merrill F. Unger, William White, and W. E. Vine. (1984). *Vine's Complete Expository Dictionary of Old and New Testament Words*. Nashville, TN: Nelson Publishers. (pp. 594-595, 466, 256-257).

Hawkins, R. E., & Clinton, T. E. (2015). *The new Christian counselor*. Harvest House Publishers. (pp. 85, 86, 243).

Miller, Stephen M. (2007). *The Complete Guide to the Bible*. Uhrichsville, Ohio: Barbour Books. (pp.386–87).

Lerner, Janet W, and Beverley H Johns. (2015). *Learning Disabilities and Related Disabilities: Strategies for Success*. Stamford, Ct: Cengage Learning. (pp. 131-135).

Thayer, Joseph Henry, Grimm Carl Ludwig Wilibald, and Christian Gottlob Wilke. (2017). *Thayer's Greek-English Lexicon of the New Testament: Coded with Strong's Concordance Numbers*. Peabody, MA: Hendrickson. (pp. 828-829, 1843).

Pearce, Michelle. (2016). *Cognitive Behavioral Therapy for Christians with Depression: A Practical Tool-Based Primer*. West Conshohocken, PA: Templeton Press. (pp. 35).

Thompson, Curt. (2010). *Anatomy of the Soul: Surprising Connections between Neuroscience and Spiritual Practices That Can Transform Your Life and Relationships.* Carol Stream, Il: Saltriver. (pp. 91, 94).

Lewis, C S. (1960) 2017. *The Four Loves.* San Francisco: Harperone.

Cloud, H., & Townsend, J. S. (2017). *Boundaries.* Zondervan. (pp.72).

APPENDIX A

A small study was completed by 56 individuals ages 13 and older specifically for education purposes. The data was collected through an anonymous Google form which participants filled out. The following data was collected and assessed:

- 53% of those who took the survey became Christians in their adolescent years (ages 5-12); 23.2% became Christians in their teen years (ages 13-19); and yet 19.6% became Christians in their young adult years (20s-30s); and surprisingly only 3.6% of those who had taken the survey became Christians in their adult years (40s or older).

- 59% of those who took the survey stated themselves as Christians for more than 20 years; 17.9% stated they were Christians for 15-19 years; 10.7% stated they were Christians for 10-14 years; 3.6% stated they were Christians for 5-9 years; and the remaining 9% had become Christians between 1 month to 4 years.

- Another 42.9% considered themselves a 'mature Christian'; 37.5% considered themselves 'Christians'; 14.3% considered themselves 'struggling Christians'; and yet 5.4% considered themselves 'baby Christians'.

This anonymous study looked at the five areas of maturity labeled by the Lifeway study mentioned earlier. Here are the results of those who considered themselves 'mature' believers.

Regularly reading the Bible. Overall, when asked how often the 56 participants read their Bible in the last year, 42.9% said they read consistently (a few times per week); 10.7% said they read consistently (once per week); 23.2% said they read a few times a month; 7.1% stated they read once per month; 16.1% said they had not read their Bible in the last year. When cross-referencing this stat about reading the Bible with the stat of those who considered themselves 'mature Christians', the statistics look different. While 58.9% considered themselves 'mature Christians', my data collections corroborate that of Lifeway. Mature believers read their Bible consistently. In fact, 70.8% of mature Christians read their Bible a few times per week, proving that consistent Bible reading and maturity have a mutual relationship, some might even say a causality.

Regularly praying: Overall, when asked how often all 56 participants prayed in the last year, 66.1% said they prayed consistently (daily); 23.2% said they prayed consistently (weekly); 10.7% said they prayed a few times a month. However, when we break down this statistic according to those who viewed themselves as 'mature Christians' we see a vast difference between labels (mature Christians) and actions (prayer). Of the mature Christians 83.3% prayed daily. That means every day! Showing once again, that there is a correlation (perhaps even a causation) between daily praying and spiritual maturity.

Serving in the church. Overall, when the 56 participants were asked how often they served in the church in the last year, 42.9% said they served consistently (a few times per week); 12.5% said they served consistently (once per week); 8.9% said they served a few times a month; 7.1% stated they served once per month; 28.6% said they had not served in the church in the last year. When we look at the data solely collected from the participants who labeled themselves as 'mature Christians' and how often they served in the church, the data once again shows a connection between being a mature believer and consistently serving in the church. 66.6% of mature believers served in the church a few times per week.

Listening to Christian music. When all 56 participants were asked how often they listened to Christian music in the last year, 37.5% said they listened exclusively to Christian music only; 33.9% said they listened mostly to Christian music; 16.1% said they listened equally to both Christian and secular music; 5.4% stated they sometimes listened to Christian music; 7.1% said they did not listen to Christian music. When we break down the statistics to take a closer look at only those that labeled themselves as 'mature Christians', the statistics of those that listen to Christian music exclusively or almost exclusively are extraordinary at 87.5%.

Missions. Overall, when all 56 participants were asked if they had ever served on a missionary trip, 19.6% responded 'yes'. 80.4% responded 'no'. Of the 19.6% that responded 'yes' they had served on a missionary trip, 29.1% of these respondents labeled themselves as a 'mature Christian', and 16.6% of these respondents labeled themselves as 'Christians'. Interestingly, 0% of those in the other groups (struggling Christians or baby Christians) had ever served on a mission trip.

Church attendance. When I asked all 56 participants how often they attended church in the last year, 58.9% said they attended consistently (a few times per week); 14.3% said they attended consistently (once per week); 10.7% said they attended a few times a month; 7.1% stated they attended once per month; 8.9% said they had not attended church in the last year. Looking at mature Christians and their church attendance, we see the following: 83.3% of those who considered themselves 'mature Christians' attend church, not just once, but rather a few times per week.

Made in the USA
Monee, IL
21 September 2024

66268816R00075